KAFFE FASSETT'S
kaleidoscope of quilts

featuring Roberta Horton • Mary Mashuta • Liza Prior Lucy
• Pauline Smith • Brandon Mably • Ruth Eglinton

A ROWAN BOOK

The Taunton Press

Shoofly Columns Quilt

 **The Taunton Press**
Inspiration for hands-on living®

The Taunton Press
63 South Main St., PO Box 5506
Newtown, CT 06470-5506
www.taunton.com

First Published in Great Britain in 2006 by Rowan Yarns

Art Director:	Kaffe Fassett
Technical editors:	Ruth Eglinton and Pauline Smith
Co-ordinator:	Pauline Smith
Editorial Director:	Kate Buller
Patchwork Designs:	Kaffe Fassett, Roberta Horton, Mary Mashuta, Liza Prior Lucy, Pauline Smith, Brandon Mably, Ruth Eglinton.
Quilters:	Judy Irish, Pauline Smith
Sewers for Liza Prior Lucy quilts:	Judy Baldwin, Corienne Kramer
Photography:	Debbie Patterson
Flat shot photography:	Dave Tolson @ Visage
Styling:	Kaffe Fassett
Design Layout:	Christine Wood - Gallery of Quilts/ front section
	Simon Wagstaff - instructions & technical information
Cover Design:	Archie Mortera
Illustrations:	Ruth Eglinton
Feature:	Kaffe Fassett

Library of Congress Cataloging-in-Publication Data

Kaffe Fassett's kaleidoscope of quilts : twenty designs from
Rowan for patchwork and quilting.
      p. cm. -- (Patchwork and quilting ; bk. 8.)
   ISBN-13: 978-1-56158-938-8
   ISBN-10: 1-56158-938-1
   1. Patchwork. 2. Quilting. I. Fassett, Kaffe. II. Title:
Kaleidoscope of quilts. III. Series.
   TT835.K337 2006
   746.46'041--dc22
                                        2006017934

Colour reproduction by Chroma Graphics (Overseas) Pte. Ltd
Printed and bound in Singapore by KHL. Printing Co. Pte. Ltd

contents

introduction

When we were thinking of locations for our next book we wanted a place with bags of colour and atmosphere, that was south of wintry England. A great friend of mine had bought and restored a 16th century tower with a walled garden on the Mediterranean island of Malta. It turned out to be the ideal choice.

The walled garden was a haven which supplied us with settings for several of our shots. The orange trees, bougainvillea and cacti combined with warm Maltese stone brought out the richness of the quilts. Then we travelled for days over potholed roads to find atmospheric old farmhouses, boats and wonderfully painted townhouses. The weather was deliciously moody – brilliant one hour soft and defused the next. We now feel we know the island and its' sister island, Gozo, very well from the point of view of locations.

Our aim was to echo or contrast with each quilt's colours to magnify the multi tones of them. I hope you agree that the old, distressed paint surfaces we discovered and the rich, weathered stone served as handsome settings for our book.

As usual we're launching new fabrics in this book. Martha Negley and Carla Miller have supplied us with wonderful designs and colourways to work with. David Wolverson, known better as a carpet designer, has joined us with a handsome collection of bas-relief tonal fabrics that are best shown in 'Tapestry Garden' and 'Deep Ohio Star.'

Banded Poppy
(Carmine colourway)
Philip Jacobs
Collection.

Philip Jacobs has also joined our design team. I've known Philip since we were young and I'd not even dreamed of designing fabric. I was totally intrigued with his work as a textile designer. At the time he was working with Ram fabrics and doing quintessentially English chintz florals that I found quite exotic. Often I would put classic, antique florals into my still life paintings at that time. Since Philip often works from old documents he catches the same mood as those flea market finds that ended up giving such a lush mood to my paintings. When we started inviting new textile artists to join me in the Rowan fabric collections I suddenly remembered my old friend and wondered if he was still doing those gorgeous upscale florals. I found him in a little farm cottage in the country he shared with his brother, painting for all the major furnishing houses in Britain. We were both delighted to work together on a patchwork collection based on his massive archive of old documents.

Banded Poppy was our first choice with its wonderful whirly movement, like Spanish dancers, the ribbon like edge giving each bloom such a distinct shape. *Pansies* came next with their strong little faces, then the classic looking *Shaggy Poppy* border fabric that took so well to colourways. A favourite has been *Trumpet Flower* with its detailed foliage and two toned blossoms. The *Coral* print I find most helpful for borders and to set off lusher prints – it has an old French feel to me. The *Geranium Leaf* print becomes a large polka dot and cuts up a treat.

In our collaboration Philip paints out the design from his reference library making the scale and density of the print to our specification, then I take the layouts to a computer expert and work out all the colourways for each print. Philip is often amazed and delighted with the results.

Kaffe Fassett

the fabrics

As a still life painter, which I was fulltime before turning to textiles, I collected copious amounts of china and decorative pots. Among these are cloisonné pieces, which are enamelled copper vessels from Eastern countries like Japan, China and Iran. Since they are made with melted glass confined to areas of the pot by small wire barriers they acquire a fine dark outline throughout the design. As I used outlines on my big new floral it had the distinct mood of cloisonné. I used colours in some of my colourways of *Cloisonné* that reflected the bright glazes found on my antique shop finds.

One of my favourite pastimes is scouring books on the decorative arts of the past or ethnic cultures to find the seed of an idea for a quilt layout or a fabric design. A woven brocade in a book on French textiles caught my eye with its bold use of lily blooms and abundant pointed leaves. With *Lilies* I tried to make the colours as saturated as possible so one ended up with a malachite green or lime fabric with highlights of colour on the flowers, the leaves and lattice background merging in tone.

When you ask an artist which is his favourite painting he is supposed to say, "a mother never admits to a favourite child" though Picasso always said "the one I'm working on now". But as I look back over my past collections I'm afraid that "Basket Of Flowers" remains a highlight. I was

OPPOSITE TOP LEFT *Shoofly Columns Quilt* showing Cloisonné border
TOP RIGHT AND BOTTOM LEFT *Tapestry Garden Quilt*
BOTTOM RIGHT *Morning Garden Quilt*

trying for the mood of those oriental carpets that employ rows upon rows of pots of flowers, repeating the same bouquet endlessly quite close together. The little auricula dotted throughout the background makes it easy to cut this dense floral for patchwork. The saturated use of colour makes most of the colourways a tonal fabric, which is easy to use. You can see in "Deep Ohio Star" it makes great borders (the top and bottom borders are fussy cut) and backing as well as being an ensemble player.

I have a Victorian print of flowers in my loo that I studied every day until the little organic dots on the petals cried out to be a fabric. At first I painted the two fabrics as one stripe that went from medium size squiggles in the *Islands* print to tiny dots in *Freckles*, creating a large stripe. Liza and Pauline felt it would be more useful to separate these so we ended up with the fine *Freckles* that is a lovely textural story and Islands that has so much atmosphere when cut. These two fabrics are shown best in my "Victorian Fans Quilt", where they make it such a mysterious arrangement of colour. You can see how well the moss colourway of *Islands* serves as a border with almost a reptilian or animal print mood to it.

Repeating flowers in Slavic embroideries inspired my *Fan Flower* design. When I was a teenager in California I was in a folk dance troupe. We researched Russian and Slavic costumes so we could embroider our own shirts. I have been fascinated by these motifs ever since.

TOP Victorian print
ABOVE *Cabin Fever Quilt* detail
RIGHT *Victorian Fans Quilt* detail

Liza's *Hazy Corners Quilt*

After years of running the first *Indian stripes* we decided a new collection was in order. This time instead of knitting out my ideas as I did for the first collection, I did small samples of each mood in petit point wool stitches on canvas. The ideas look more like weaving so we could tell better what we'd end up with. I went for a simpler more saturated look so that the fabrics can be used as a textured solid or as a subtle stripe. Some we did with a more pronounced contrast, so these appear more stripy. Liza's "Hazy Corners" is a superb sampler of most of the moods that the hand weavers achieved.

I've done several second versions of some of my quilts to demonstrate how one can take a particular layout and transform it by using a different palette and mood of fabrics. After "Deep Ohio Star" with its deep floral and fruit prints I wanted to see this layout of stars with a different border in a far softer pastel palette. I used a new fabric that is close to my heart, *Harvest Toile*, in fuchsia colourway as a constant ground print. Then I checkerboarded

chalky, pastel stars with this magenta pink base to create a much lighter quilt.

Kaffe's Pastel Ohio Star Quilt

The "Pinwheel" also gets a light and dark treatment, the pastel one looking quite vintage. I often like a very merging palette but "Pinwheel" needs a certain amount of contrast to make it work. With the "Cool Diamonds" quilts I took all the cool blues, lavenders and soft greens, whereas the "Hot Diamonds" is like a rich fruit salad saturated in berry juices. I always begin by arranging the pieces on a design wall, making changes and fine tuning until I'm happy with the arrangement. It's a good idea to stand back to take a look. I use a reducing glass so I can see the whole layout in a glance. It's easier to remove pieces that don't work now rather than using a seam ripper.

I look forward to seeing all the versions you come up with for each and everyone of the quilts in this book.

Bottle Pinwheel Quilt by Kaffe Fassett
I love the way my *Bottle Pinwheel* is framed by the arched gateway and architectural planting.

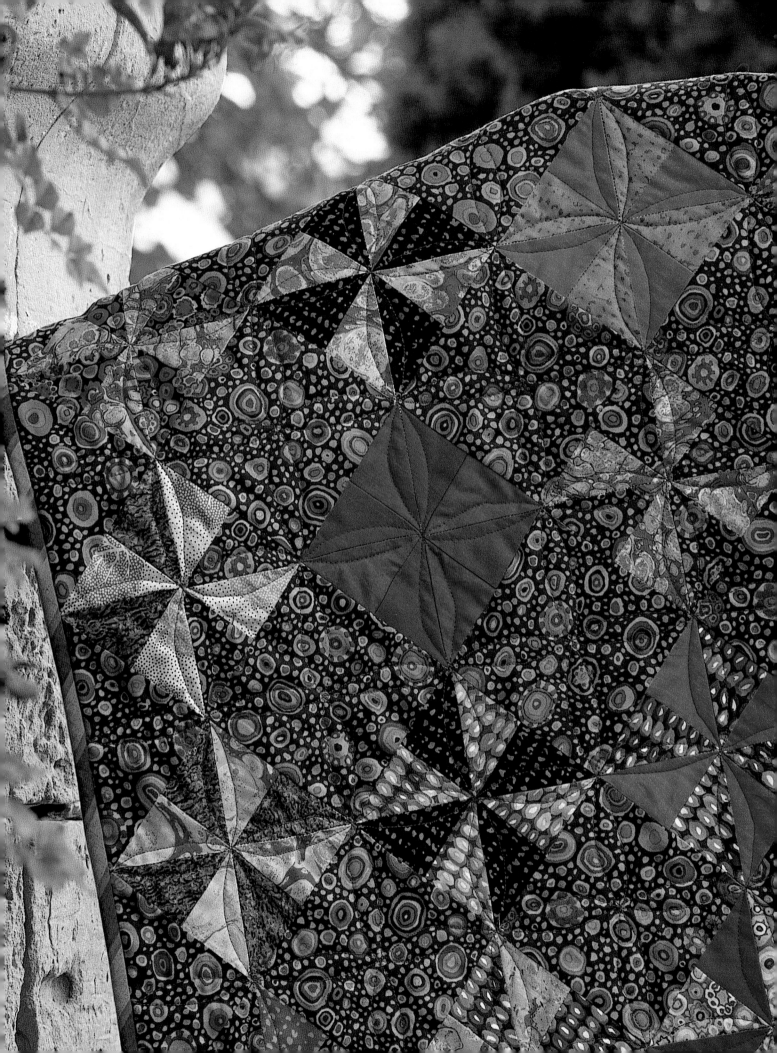

Broken Dishes Quilt by Kaffe Fassett
Broken Dishes with Zurrieq church at sunset. The detail shows the pieced backing and scrap binding.

Cabin Fever Quilt by Kaffe Fassett
My *Cabin Fever* using mostly small, textural prints is bordered with Islands and backed with Burntwood Rose.

Cool Diamonds Quilt by Kaffe Fassett
The cool duck egg blues and lavenders looking lush with bougainvillea vine.
My Embroidered Leaf makes a great backing.

Deep Ohio Star Quilt by Kaffe Fassett
Rich, jewel coloured stars are bordered by Basket Of Flowers print. I like the way
the quilt is hanging from the 16th century tower.

Pastel Ohio Star Quilt by Kaffe Fassett
The vibrant pastels in this quilt
work a treat with the golden walls
and pink door. The boy in his
green top is the finishing touch.
The quilt also looks good against
the rusty boat.

24

Spools Quilt by Pauline Smith
As I spotted the blue and yellow boats at Pretty Bay I knew I'd found
the setting for Pauline's *Spools Quilt*.

Moonflowers Quilt by Ruth Eglinton
An interesting, small project featuring many of Martha Negley
florals, Ruth's *Moonflowers Quilt*, looks good here.

Morning Garden Quilt by Kaffe Fassett
With its high pastel palette, *Morning Garden* looks at home on this elegant old building.

Hazy Corners Quilt by Liza Prior Lucy
The indian woven stripes of Liza's *Hazy Corners Quilt* looks gorgeous with the strong colours of the boat.

Little Boxes Quilt by Pauline Smith
I love the way Pauline's *Little Boxes*, with its glowing Matisse palette, looks in this boat.

Matisse Villa Quilt by Roberta Horton
Roberta's *Matisse Villa* looks stunning against the golden stone of a tomb in this Maltese cemetery.

New Orleans Star Quilt by Liza Prior Lucy
The colours of storms, oil slicks and dark waters in Liza's *New Orleans Star* reflect all the tones of this Valletta street.

Rustic Snowballs Quilt by Brandon Mably
Brandon's *Rustic Snowballs* looking quite architectural against the

Shoofly Columns Quilt by Kaffe Fassett
The gates of an Art Nouveau style villa were the perfect spot to hang my *Shoofly Columns*. The quilt is backed with my Cabbage&Roses fabric.

Tapestry Garden Quilt by Kaffe Fassett
The rich, earthy palette I've used in *Tapestry Garden* shows up well against the old, green door in Valletta. The detail shows David Wolverson Bas-Relief fabric.

Victorian Fans Quilt by Kaffe Fassett
I used mostly Freckles and Islands prints in this quilt. The outer border of rust Lava print
goes so well with the lichen covered stone.

Pastel Pinwheel Quilt by Kaffe Fassett
This could so easily be one of my still life paintings with my *Pastel Pinwheel Quilt* and the painted enamelware

Told You So Baskets Quilt by Mary Mashuta
With simple elegance Mary's *Told You So Baskets* glows here in a Maltese garden.

mary mashuta

fabric and color — too much is not enough

Living in the San Francisco Bay Area is the perfect place for me. There are wonderful places to visit, lots of beautiful weather, great food, and a huge quilt community. California quilters love color and are adventurous and eager to try new things. Another added bonus for me is that I live with my twin, and fellow quilter, Roberta Horton. (She also designs for Rowan and was the featured artist in the third book of this series.)

Roberta and I maintain separate home studios and fabric stashes. Occasionally we share our fabrics, but I will have to confess to getting in trouble a couple of times for not asking first! You will have to admit it would be tempting to have another quilt stash so readily available twenty-four hours a day, rain or shine, that you can access even in your jammies. We tend to go our own way when we design quilts. It's delicious to start work on a new one when the other one is out of town teaching. Roberta said it all when she commented, "I occasionally ask Mary her opinion on one of my quilts. Oddly enough, as soon as I hear her thoughts, I know I want just the opposite". Our mom taught us to sew. We graduated from doll clothes to making our own wardrobes. I have always loved fabric so it was easy to switch from making clothes to creating wearable art and quilts.

Two degrees in Home Economics and a teaching credential gave me the formal background to teach and to work in the interior design field. Even though I have had a lot of art history and decorative arts classes, working in design provided me with the opportunity to try out new color schemes, work with fabrics that weren't necessarily my favorites, and expand my horizons. I even got paid to practice. I have included a few pictures of our house to show you that I still enjoy decorating.

In interior design I learned about co-ordinated fabric collections. These were sets of fabric that were specifically designed to go together because they had a common theme or "feeling" and were colored with the same set of dyes. There were usually two or three prints, a number of solids, and possibly a stripe, plaid, or a dot. We find the same thing in quilt fabric collections. I also learned that fabrics came in multiple colorways, which are just different color versions of the same design. Again, this also applies to quilt fabrics. I think that fabric collections often tempt quilters because they know their quilt will be color co-ordinated. I don't think most work with colorways other than selecting which is their favorite color from the set and then picking the other designs to match. The whole process can be very comforting to beginning quilters.

My approach to fabric selection is a little different. My own fabric collections are built on like subject matter (food, cats, Christmas, Halloween) or fabric type (stripes, dots,

1 What fun to still cook on the 1927 Spark stove that came with our 1913 house. I am wearing an apron made from a feed sack and many sizes of red gingham.

2 Never tell me I can pick any color I want to refinish a tub or that I can have any hexagon tile floor design I want.

3 My bedroom is an eclectic mix: a Scottish bed with a Chinese tie-dye spread, an Amish quilt, and a hand painted cabinet from New Mexico. The small quilt is one of my first.

solids, feed sacks). I am entertained by seeing how fabrics that weren't necessarily made for each other end up working together. Slightly mismatching can be fun and much more lively and artful. I often buy multiple colorways of a fabric if I like the design enough. In recent years I have challenged myself to see how many of the set I could include in the same quilt. The consistent design pattern pulls the quilt together, but the different colors stir it up again.

My current quilt, *Told You So Baskets*, uses two colorways of a floral and three colorways of a stripe. A great number of my quilts do contain stripes including the five I have designed for Rowan. Again, looking at *Told You So Baskets*, you can see that the stripes can play various roles. They are a major design element in the baskets and an accessory, supportive feature in the alternate squares which are my favorite part of the quilt since I had never tried this before. I often pick a stripe for the binding because even this minor part of the quilt makes its contribution. Here the bias-cut stripe raises the activity level because it helps to draw the viewer's eye around the quilt.

I have enjoyed working with Kaffe's fabrics over the years because there always are so many designs to select from. I am not limited to one co-ordinated collection. Often the color combinations in a print or stripe aren't ones I could possibly come up with on my own, but they are always luscious and exciting. The day the new Rowan samples arrive at our house is special indeed. I usually have several possible blocks in mind to "shop" for, or sometimes a special new fabric inspires me to search for a new block altogether. With both of us looking at the fabrics, it is usually a matter of first "dibs", or staking out an important fabric for yourself. I gravitate toward relatively simple pieced blocks because showcasing the fabric is what is important to me. Once I discover a new block and have begun to understand it, numerous ways of using it come to mind; "What if I used these fabrics?" "What if I arranged the blocks in that way instead?" You can call this working in a "series" because multiple quilts are created that have at least one thing in common, in this case the block. I think of it as getting a lot of mileage out of the block. It's also fun to see what my students do with my block.

Over the years I have created many quilts. My work runs the gamut from very serious, competition-worthy quilts to simplified versions of major quilts that I use as teaching examples. I have three goals for my quilt making: learn something new from each quilt, be open to learn from my students, and to enjoy the journey. I am always interested in how other quilters approach design. I have paired some of my quilts so you can see how my work relates to itself.

4 *Square Dots* 63in x 62in 2003.

5 *Dot.Dot.Dot* 62in x 61in 1999.

6 *Trumpet Vine* 59in x 59in 1997.

I have challenged myself to make quilts with just one fabric type. Here are two of a series of all-dot quilts. I used the simple Square within Square block for *Square Dots*. I was able to use three colorways of an incredibly large dot design when I cheated and used the third for the back. The fabric was purchased for an ill-fated wearable art ensemble, but after Roberta said it would look like clown pajamas the idea was ruined for me. The square blocks were cut from three sets of dot fabrics: 16 pink, 16 aqua, and 16 yellow. Obviously, I would rather have a bit of many fabrics rather than a lot of just a few.

Dot.Dot.Dot is a more sophisticated all-dot quilt. I used the Circle within Circle block. (An appliquéd version of this block was selected for *Hazy Sunshine* in series #4.) There are many possible layouts for the segments of the block with this serpentine one being the hardest to work out. I combined vintage, feed sack, and contemporary dots. The fabrics were randomly cut and placed, but then I rearranged the corner "L" shaped pieces in color flows by row to give more order to the composition. Since I don't sew any block until the whole composition is worked out on my design wall it was easy to refine the composition.

I created the two template Serpentine Curves block to show off stripes. In *Trumpet Vine*. The blocks are arranged in a very contemporary setting with stripes being repeated from one block to the next in multiples that keep drawing the eye around the quilt. It was the first time I used Kaffe's stripes in a quilt, you can see how well they contrast and add variety to the mix of other stripes from my collection. The quilt was selected for Quilt Visions which is an international art quilt show. Much to my dismay, Roberta told me to get rid of one multiple-colorway stripe in *Trumpet Vine* while I was working on it. She was right for once! However, the rejected pieces combined perfectly with vegetable prints that had also been eliminated. *Mixed Greens* has a totally different, more traditional layout. It was part of the Women of Taste show which paired women quilters with women chefs. The Smithsonian Museum in Washington D.C. toured the show to a number of venues.

I also enjoy playing within the confines of a sashed grid. I divide the quilt into "zones" thus limiting what fabric type can go where. Once that decision is made, I can play with just one area of the quilt while I am composing it. Both of these quilts allowed me to use lots of different fabrics which is what I really love to do.

Stripe Posy Patch is made entirely from American feed sacks which are "utility" bags that came into use after the Civil War and were popular through the 1950s. They were produced to package grains, human foods, and livestock feeds. Somewhere along the way the manufacturers realized that the farmers' wives would be attracted to the printed bags as they could be recycled into household and clothing items. I was first attracted to the sacks because of the wonderful stripes which patterned many of them. Strangely enough, most other quilters buy the prints and stay away from the stripes. I have to force myself to buy the prints. The Posy Patch block is huge and it took only nine blocks to make the quilt. That meant that I could showcase nine sets of fabric: one stripe and eight prints in each.

7 *Mixed Greens* 57in x 57in. 1998.

Harajuku Street Fashion is a much more complicated grid, or sashed quilt. It was inspired by the kids who hang out in the Harajuku section of Tokyo on Sundays. Their creative clothing ensembles mix East and West in unexpected ways. Who would have guessed I could combine summer kimono yukata, 1960s San Francisco "Summer of Love" hippy fabrics, and sophisticated Japanese stripes and vintage Aizome in the same quilt? "Finder's keepers!" was the verdict when I rediscovered Roberta's paste resist Aizome in the basement. It made a calming border fabric. What a 'far out' quilt and unusual juxtaposition of fabrics. I seriously doubt any Japanese quilter would have come up with this particular combination of fabrics.

In all my quilts, I pick a block, select and amass fabrics, my assistant Rebecca Rohrcaste rotary cuts the pieces, and I place them on my design wall. Once there, the pieces are moved around, contemplated, and adjusted. THEN, as previously mentioned, I sew the quilt together, block by block and row by row. My method works for me since I use so many different fabrics and may want to audition them in several locations. There is no ripping involved, and I am always happy with the end results.

8 *Stripe Posy Patch* 60in x 60in 2000.

I mentioned working in the interior design field in the beginning of this article. I'm a full-time quilter now so I don't do that anymore. However, I do work with quilters in designing their studios, or workspaces, and that is very rewarding. I have learned that no matter how small or large the space is, a quilter can always fill it with fabric and still want more room.

All photos by Sharon Risedorph except no. 3 by author.

9 *Harajuku Street Fashion* 73in x 73in 2004.

Hot Diamonds Quilt ★★

Kaffe Fassett

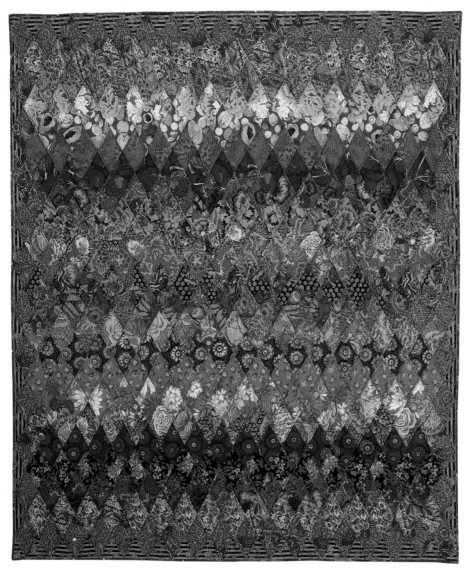

In my first book, 'Glorious Patchwork' I did a version of Red Diamonds that proved to be a very popular quilt. When I realized we had so many larger scale floral and vegetable prints in a rusty red range I felt it time to do a fresh version of this old favourite.

SIZE OF QUILT
The finished quilt will measure approx.
108in x 93½in (274cm x 237.5cm).

MATERIALS
Patchwork Fabrics:

ZINNIA

Antique	GP31AN: ½ yd (45cm)	
Crimson	GP31CR: ½ yd (45cm)	

KIMONO
Crimson/Magenta	GP33CM: ½ yd (45cm)

Rust/Purple	GP33RP: ½ yd (45cm)	

CABBAGE & ROSES
Rustic	GP38RC: ½ yd (45cm)
Wine	GP38WN: 1 yd (90cm)

ROMANY
Jewel	GP39JW: 1 yd (90cm)
Red	GP39RD: ½ yd (45cm)

LILIES
Magenta	GP45MG: ½ yd (45cm)

CLOISONNE
Magenta	GP46MG: ½ yd (45cm)

Teal	GP46TE: 1 yd (90cm)

BURNT WOOD ROSE
Wine	GP47WN: 1⅝ yds (1.5m)

FLOWER BASKET
Black	GP48BK: ½ yd (45cm)

FLOWER SPRAYS
Black	LC01BK: ½ yd (45cm)

HYDRANGEA
Black	LC02BK: 1 yd (90cm)

ARBOUR
Tobacco	LC05TO: ½ yd (45cm)

VEGETABLE LEAVES
Red	MN05RD: ½ yd (45cm)

DAHLIA
Summer Delight	MN06SD: ½ yd (45cm)

MARIGOLD
Red	MN07RD: ½ yd (45cm) or use leftover from backing.

FRUIT
Red	MN09RD: ½ yd (45cm)

Backing Fabric: 8½ yds (7.8m)
We suggest these fabrics for backing:
VEGETABLE DOT, Red MN02RD
MARIGOLD, Red MN07RD
Leftover backing fabric can be used in the quilt. Whilst the VEGETABLE DOT fabric is not used in the quilt it could be substituted for any of the red toned print fabrics.

Binding:
VEGETABLE LEAVES
Red	MN05RD: ¾ yd (70cm)

Batting:
116 x 101in (294.5cm x 256.5cm).

Quilting thread:
Claret hand or machine quilting thread.

Templates:
see pages 116, 117

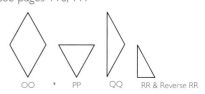

PATCH SHAPES
The quilt made up of one diamond patch shape (Template OO) and three triangle patch shapes (PP, QQ and RR & Reverse RR) which are used to fill in around the edges of the quilt.

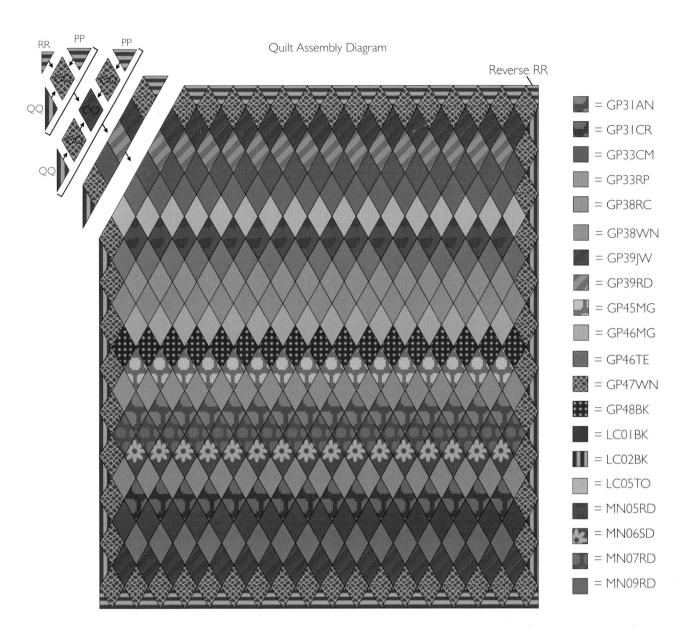

Quilt Assembly Diagram

Reverse RR

= GP31AN
= GP31CR
= GP33CM
= GP33RP
= GP38RC
= GP38WN
= GP39JW
= GP39RD
= GP45MG
= GP46MG
= GP46TE
= GP47WN
= GP48BK
= LC01BK
= LC02BK
= LC05TO
= MN05RD
= MN06SD
= MN07RD
= MN09RD

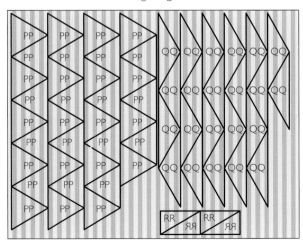

Cutting Diagram

CUTTING OUT

Template OO: Cut 5in (12.75cm) wide strips across the width of the fabric. Each strip will give you 6 patches per 45in (114cm) wide fabric. Cut 56 in GP47WN, 34 in GP38WN, GP39JW, 33 in GP46TE, 17 in GP33CM, GP38RC, GP48BK, LC01BK, LC05TO, MN07RD, 16 in GP31AN, GP31CR, GP33RP, GP39RD, GP45MG, GP46MG, MN05RD, MN06SD and MN09RD.

Template PP, QQ, RR & reverse RR: All cut in fabric LC02BK. The stripe direction is important for these patch shapes. They are cut from the length of the fabric, refer to the cutting diagram for template layout. Cut 34 Template PP triangles, 22 Template QQ triangles, 2 Template RR triangles, then flip the template over and cut 2 Template reverse RR triangles in LC02BK.

Binding: cut 10 strips 2½in (6.5cm) wide × width of fabric in MN05RD.

Backing: Cut 2 pieces 101in × 44in (256.5cm by 112cm) and 1 piece 101in × 29in (256.5cm × 73.5cm) in backing fabric.

MAKING THE QUILT
Using a ¼in (6mm) seam allowance throughout, join the template OO diamond patches into diagonal rows, filling in along the top edge of the quilt with template PP triangles, the sides of the quilt with template QQ triangles and the extreme corners with templates RR & reverse RR, as shown in the quilt assembly diagram. Refer to the quilt assembly diagram for fabric sequence, laying each row out in turn will help to keep the fabric sequence correct.

FINISHING THE QUILT
Press the quilt top. Seam the backing pieces using a ¼in (6mm) seam allowance to form a piece approx. 116 × 101in (294.5cm × 256.5cm). Layer the quilt top, batting and backing and baste together (see page 122). Using claret thread, quilt in a diamond checkerboard pattern. Each line of quilting is offset by ¼in (6mm) on each side of the seam lines, this can be done by hand or machine. Trim the quilt edges and attach the binding (see page 122).

Cool Diamonds Quilt ★★

KAFFE FASSETT

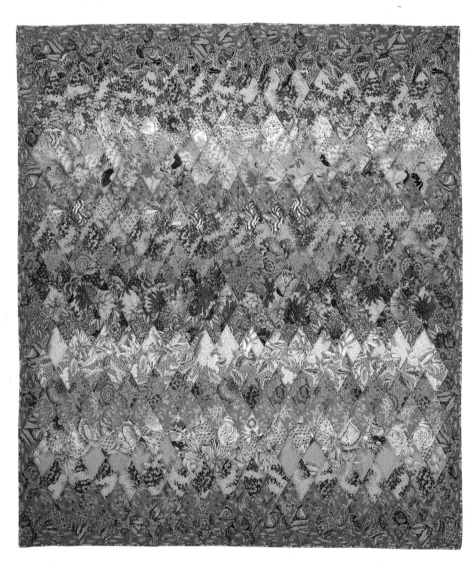

Here I've taken the same layout as Hot Diamonds but done it in all the duck egg hues, lavenders and magenta fabrics, the result is a cool rippling of leaves and blossoms that is quite lush.

SIZE OF QUILT
The finished quilt will measure approx. 108in × 93½in (274cm × 237.5cm).

MATERIALS
Patchwork Fabrics:
HARVEST TOILE
Fuchsia   GP35FU: ½ yd (45cm)
Teal   GP35TE: ½ yd (45cm)
CABBAGE & ROSES
Cerulean   GP38CE: ½ yd (45cm)
Spring   GP38SP: 1 yd (90cm)
EMBROIDERED LEAF
Pink   GP42PK: ½ yd (45cm)
Taupe   GP42TA: ½ yd (45cm) or
                       use leftover from backing.

LILIES
Malachite   GP45MA: 1⅝ yds (1.5m)
CLOISONNE
Aqua   GP46AQ: 1 yd (90cm)
BURNT WOOD ROSE
Moss   GP47MS: ½ yd (90cm)
FLOWER BASKET
Duck Egg   GP48DE: ½ yd (45cm)
FLOWER SPRAYS
Sage   LC01SA: 1 yd (90cm)
Taupe   LC01TA: ½ yd (45cm)
HYDRANGEA
Green   LC02GN: 1 yd (90cm)
ARBOUR
Duck Egg   LC05DE: 1 yd (90cm)
Green   LC05GN: ½ yd (45cm)
Pink   LC05PK: ½ yd (45cm)
DAHLIA
Purple   MN06PU: ½ yd (45cm)
FRUITS & FLORALS
Purple   MN08PU: ½ yd (45cm) or
                       use leftover from backing.
PLUMERIA
Purple   MN10PU: ½ yd (45cm)

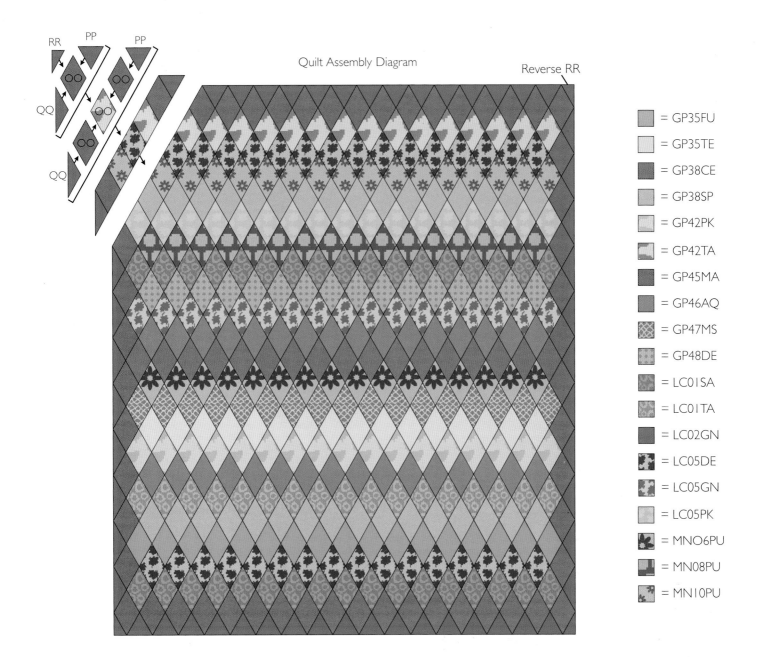

Quilt Assembly Diagram

Backing Fabric: 8½ yds (7.8m)
We suggest these fabrics for backing:
EMBROIDERED LEAF, Taupe GP42TA
FRUITS & FLORALS, Purple MN08PU
Leftover backing fabric can be used in the quilt.

Binding:
PLUMERIA
Purple   MN10PU: ¾ yd (70cm)

Batting:
116 × 101in (294.5cm × 256.5cm).

Quilting thread:
Soft grey hand or machine quilting thread.

Templates:
See Hot Diamonds Quilt.

PATCH SHAPES
See Hot Diamonds Quilt.

CUTTING OUT
Template OO: Cut 5in (12.75cm) wide strips
across the width of the fabric. Each strip will
give you 6 patches per 45in (114cm) wide
fabric. Cut 56 in GP45MA, 34 in LC01SA 32
in GP38SP, GP46AQ, LC05DE, 17 in
GP35FU, GP38CE, GP42PK, GP42TA,
GP47MS, LC01TA, LC05GN, LC05PK,
MN10PU, 16 in GP35TE, GP48DE, MN06PU
and MN08PU.
Template PP, QQ, RR & reverse RR: All cut
in fabric LC02GN. The stripe direction is
important for these patch shapes. They are
cut from the length of the fabric, refer to the
cutting diagram on page 51 for template

layout. Cut 34 Template PP triangles, 22
Template QQ triangles, 2 Template RR
triangles, then flip the template over and cut
2 Template reverse RR triangles in LC02GN.

Binding: cut 10 strips 2½in (6.5cm) wide ×
width of fabric in MN10PU.

Backing: Cut 2 pieces 101in × 44in
(256.5cm by 112cm) and 1 piece 101in ×
29in (256.5cm × 73.5cm) in backing fabric.

MAKING THE QUILT
See Hot Diamonds Quilt instructions.

FINISHING THE QUILT
See Hot Diamonds Quilt instructions.

= GP35FU
= GP35TE
= GP38CE
= GP38SP
= GP42PK
= GP42TA
= GP45MA
= GP46AQ
= GP47MS
= GP48DE
= LC01SA
= LC01TA
= LC02GN
= LC05DE
= LC05GN
= LC05PK
= MN06PU
= MN08PU
= MN10PU

Victorian Fans Quilt ★★

KAFFE FASSETT

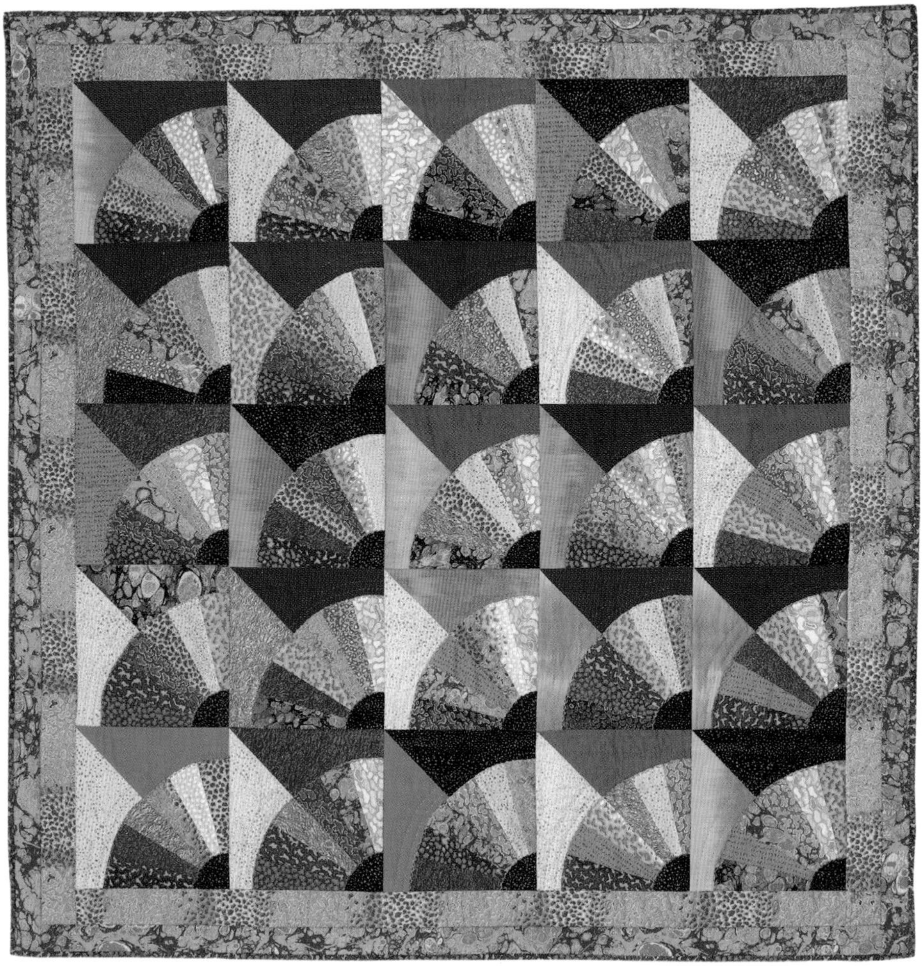

I've always wanted to do a fans quilt having bought a couple of 'flour sack' quilts made in the 1930s. I spotted a deep, rich one in a collection of antique quilts and found my new FRECKLES and ISLANDS prints perfect in their colourings to do my version.

SIZE OF QUILT
The finished quilt will measure approx. 65in x 65in (165cm x 165cm).

MATERIALS
Note: The Islands fabric has distinct design elements printed in stripes across the width of the fabric, please refer to the photograph for guidance.

Patchwork Fabrics:

LAVA
Rust CM01RU: ¾ yd (70cm)
Includes borders
Turquoise CM01TQ: ⅜ yd (35cm)
FOSSIL
Blue CM03BL: ⅜ yd (35cm)
Rust CM03RU: ⅜ yd (35cm)
CHICKEN SCRATCH
Turquoise CM05TQ: ⅜ yd (35cm)
FRECKLES
Bottle GP40BT: ¾ yd (70cm)
Gold GP40GD: ⅜ yd (35cm)
Pink GP40PK: ⅜ yd (35cm)
CAMOUFLAGE
Pearl GP44PR: ⅜ yd (35cm)
ISLANDS
Bottle GP49BT: ½ yd (45cm)
Gold GP49GD: ⅝ yd (60cm)
Moss GP49MS: 1⅞ yds (1.7m)
Includes borders
Pink GP49PK: ⅜ yd (35cm)
Rust GP49RU: ⅜ yd (35cm)
SHOT COTTON
Ginger SC01: ⅜ yd (35cm)
Cassis SC02: ⅜ yd (35cm)
Prune SC03: ⅜ yd (35cm)
Slate SC04: ⅜ yd (35cm)
Lavender SC14: ⅜ yd (35cm)
Smoky SC20: ⅜ yd (35cm)
Charcoal SC25: ⅜ yd (35cm)
SINGLE IKAT WASH
Banana SIW03: ⅜ yd (35cm)
Red SIW06: ⅜ yd (35cm)

Border Fabrics:

LAVA
Rust CM01RU:
see patchwork fabrics
ISLANDS
Moss GP49MS:
see patchwork fabrics

Backing Fabric: 4⅛ yds (3.8m)
We suggest these fabrics for backing:
FLOWER BASKET, Rust GP48RU
CAMOUFLAGE, Pearl GP44PR
LAVA, Turquoise CM01TQ

Binding:
ISLANDS
Bottle GP49BT: ½ yd (45cm)

Batting:
73in x 73in (186 x 186cm).

Quilting and Embroidery thread:
Perlé cotton in bright pink, lime, gold and blue.

Templates:
See pages 107, 115

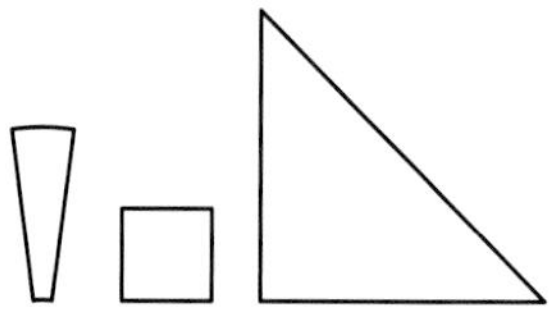

PATCH SHAPES
This quilt is made from blocks pieced using 1 large triangle patch shape (cut to size) and 1 square patch shape (Template K). Each block has an appliquéd fan made up from a fan segment patch shape (Template J). The quilt is finished with an inner and outer border.

Quilt Assembly Diagram

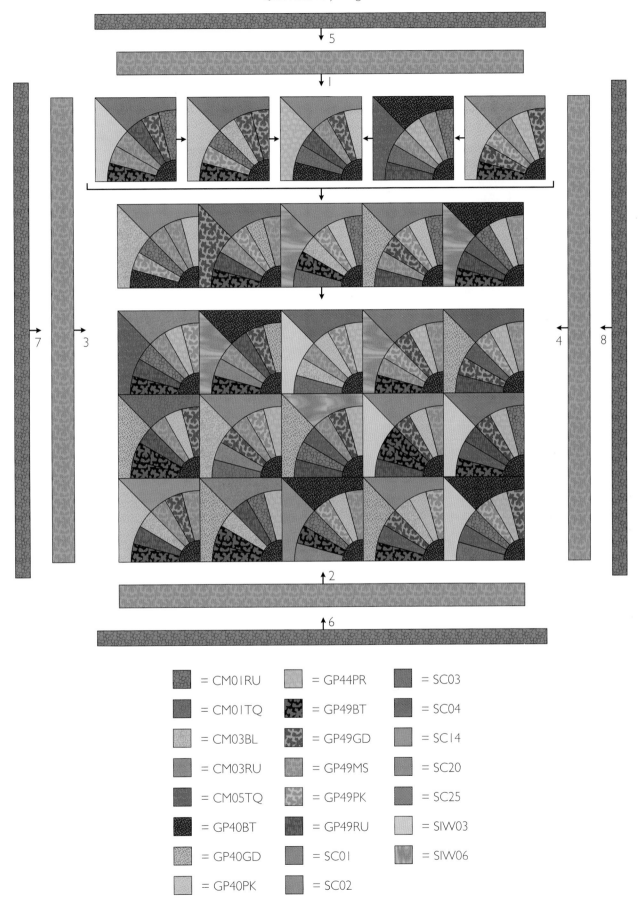

= CM01RU		= GP44PR		= SC03
= CM01TQ		= GP49BT		= SC04
= CM03BL		= GP49GD		= SC14
= CM03RU		= GP49MS		= SC20
= CM05TQ		= GP49PK		= SC25
= GP40BT		= GP49RU		= SIW03
= GP40GD		= SC01		= SIW06
= GP40PK		= SC02		

CUTTING OUT

Note: The ISLANDS fabric has design elements printed in stripes across the width of the fabric. Therefore, cut the inner borders first and then use the remaining fabric to cut other patch shapes.

Inner Border: Cut 2 strips 61½in x 3½in (156.25cm x 9cm) and 2 strips 55½in x 31½ in (141cm x 9cm) down the length of the fabric in GP49MS. Reserve the remaining fabric for Template J.

Outer Border: Cut 6 strips 2½in (6.5cm) x the width of the fabric, join as necessary and cut 2 strips 65½in x 2½in (166.5cm x 6.5cm) and 2 strips 61½in x 2½in (156.25cm x 6.5cm) in CM01RU.

Large Triangles: Cut 11⅞in (30.25cm) wide strips across the width of the fabric. Each strip will give you 6 patches per 45in (114cm) wide fabric. Cut 11⅞in (30.25cm) squares, cut each square diagonally to form 2 triangles. Cut 6 triangles in GP40GD, 5 in GP40BT, SIW03, SIW06, 4 in SC02, 3 in CM03RU, GP40PK, SC03, 2 in CM03BL, CM05TQ, SC04, SC14, SC20, SC25, 1 in CM01TQ, GP44PR, GP49GD and SC01. Reserve leftover strips for Template J.

Template J: We recommend making a plastic template for the fan shape. For the ISLANDS fabrics fussy cut by drawing around the template to take advantage of the different design elements.

For all other fabrics cut 7¼in (18.5cm) wide strips across the width of the fabric. Each strip will give you 18 patches per 45in (114cm) wide fabric. Place the template on the strip with the grain line vertical and draw around the shape. Rotate the template 180° and draw the next shape alongside the first with the side cutting lines touching, carry on adding more shapes in the same way until you have the required number. Cut the shapes apart, then trim the curves top and bottom accurately. Cut 25 in GP49MS, 19 in GP49BT, 18 in GP49GD, 15 in GP49RU, 14 in GP49PK, 13 in CM01RU, 11 in GP44PR, 10 in GP40PK, 6 in CM01TQ, CM03BL, CM05TQ, 3 in CM03RU, 2 in GP40GD and GP40BT.

Template K: Cut 3½in (9cm) wide strips across the width of the fabric. Each strip will give you 12 patches per 45in (114cm) wide fabric. Cut 25 in GP40BT.

Binding: Cut 7 strips 2½in (6.5cm) wide x width of fabric in GP49BT.

Backing: Cut 1 piece 44in x 73in (112cm x 186cm) and 1 piece 30in x 73in (76cm x 186cm) in backing fabric.

MAKING THE BLOCKS

Use a ¼in (6mm) seam allowance throughout and refer to the quilt assembly diagram for fabric placement. Take the large triangle patch shapes and piece 25 blocks as shown in block assembly diagram a. Take 1 block and a template K square, both right sides up, place the square on the corner of the block matching the raw edges carefully, pin in place as shown in diagram b.

Take 6 fan segments (Template J) and piece together as shown in diagram c to form the fan shape. Note: For the Islands fabrics, where 2 segments are shown to be adjacent in the quilt assembly diagram use different design elements. Carefully press a ¼in (6mm) seam allowance along the curved edges of the fan.

Layer the fan onto the block as shown in diagram d. Baste the fan into place and then stitch into place using decorative herringbone embroidery stitch. Use perlé cotton in bright pink, lime, gold and blue for the embroidery. Finally, trim away excess fabric from behind the appliquéd fan shape leaving a ¼in (6mm) seam allowance.

MAKING THE QUILT

Join the blocks into 5 rows of 5 blocks then join the rows to form the quilt centre. Add the inner and outer borders in the order indicated in the quilt assembly diagram.

FINISHING THE QUILT

Press the quilt top. Seam the backing pieces using a ¼in (6mm) seam allowance to form a piece approx. 73in x 73in (186cm x 186cm). Layer the quilt top, batting and backing and baste together (see page 122). Hand quilt lines around the curve of each fan using Perlé cotton in bright pink, lime, gold and blue. Trim the quilt edges and attach the binding (see page 122).

Block Assembly Diagrams

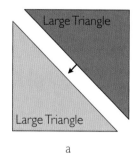

a

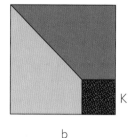

b

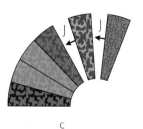

c

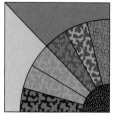

d

Shoofly Columns Quilt ★★

KAFFE FASSETT

Yet another traditional block that has caught my eye for some years. It has a masculine chunkiness in our new brown palette. Up scale prints work so well in the columns.

SIZE OF QUILT
The finished quilt will measure approx.
85in x 75½in (216cm x 192cm).

MATERIALS
Patchwork Fabrics:
AWNING STRIPE
Lilac	AWS04: ¼ yd (25cm)
Brown	AWS05: ¼ yd (25cm)
Midnight	AWS06: ¼ yd (25cm)

BATIK CONFETTI
Moss	BKC03: ¼ yd (25cm)

LAVA
Rust	CM01RU: 1½yds (1.4m)

MARBLE
Blue	CM02BL: ¼ yd (25cm)
Fuchsia	CM02FU: ¼ yd (25cm)
Pink	CM02PK: ¼ yd (25cm)
Turquoise	CM02TQ: ¼ yd (25cm)

FOSSIL
Turquoise	CM03TQ: ¼ yd (25cm)

PAPERWEIGHT
Sludge	GP20SL: ¼ yd (25cm)

FAN FLOWERS
Ochre	GP36OC: 1 yd (90cm)

CLOISONNE
Moss	GP46MS: 2½yds (2.1m)

WOVEN HAZE STRIPE
Persimmon	HZS01: ¼ yd (25cm)
Terracotta	HZS10: ¼ yd (25cm)
Denim Blue	HZS15: ¼ yd (25cm)

SINGLE IKAT FEATHERS
Curry	SIF01: ¼ yd (25cm)
Earth	SIF02: ¼ yd (25cm)

Backing Fabric: 5¼ yds (4.7m)
We suggest these fabrics for backing:
CABBAGE & ROSES, Wood GP38WD
WOVEN HAZE STRIPE, Terracotta HZS10
SINGLE IKAT FEATHERS, Earth SIF02.

Binding:
BEAD STRIPE
Jungle   GP50JG: ¾ yd (70cm)

Batting:
93in x 83in (236cm x 211cm).

Quilting thread:
Ochre machine quilting thread.

Templates:
see pages 107, 113 ,114

PATCH SHAPES

Shoofly blocks made using 1 square patch
shape (Template B) and 1 triangle patch
shape (Template LL) are set 'on point' into
columns using 2 triangle patch shapes
(Templates MM and NN). You'll find half
template MM on page 114. Take a large piece
of paper, fold, place the edge of template
MM to the fold of paper, trace around shape
and cut out. Open out for the complete
template. The pieced columns are
interspaced with 4 sashing strips, 2 narrow
between the columns and 2 wide on the
outside edges of the quilt.

CUTTING OUT

Template B: Cut 2½in (6.5cm) wide strips
across the width of the fabric. Each strip will
give you 16 patches per 45in (114cm) wide
fabric. Cut 16 in SIF01, 15 in BKC03,
CM02BL, CM02FU, GP20SL, 12 in HZS10,
10 in CM02PK, CM02TQ, CM03TQ, 8 in
AWS04, AWS05, AWS06, HZS01, SIF02
and 4 in HZS15.

Template LL: Cut 4⅞in (12.5cm) wide strips
across the width of the fabric. Each strip will
give you 16 patches per 45in (114cm) wide
fabric. Cut 16 in SIF01, 12 in BKC03,
CM02BL, CM02FU, GP20SL, HZS10, 8 in
AWS04, AWS05, AWS06, CM02PK,
CM02TQ, CM03TQ, HZS01, SIF02 and 4 in
HZS15.

Template MM: Cut 7¾in (19.75cm) wide
strips across the width of the fabric. Each
strip will give you 4 patches per 45in
(114cm) wide fabric. Place the template with
the long side along the cut edge of the strip,
this will ensure the long side of the triangles
will not have a bias edge. Cut 20 in CM01RU
and 10 in GP36OC.

Template NN: Cut 8in (20.25cm) wide strips
across the width of the fabric. Each strip will
give you 10 patches per 45in (114cm) wide
fabric. Cut 8 in CM01RU and 4 in GP36OC.

Sashing: From the length of the fabric cut
2 strips 86in x 10in (218.5cm x 25.5cm) and
2 strips 86in x 7½in (218.5cm x 19cm).
These strips are cut a little longer than
necessary and will be trimmed to fit.

Binding: Cut 14 strips 2½in (6.5cm) wide
down the length of the fabric in GP50JG. Join
the strips to form a binding approx. 9¼yds
(8.5m) in length. Extra fabric has been

allowed for matching.

Backing: Cut 2 pieces 42in x 93in
(106.5cm x 236cm) in backing fabric.

MAKING THE BLOCKS AND PIECED COLUMNS

Use a ¼in (6mm) seam allowance
throughout. Piece 18 blocks following block
assembly diagram a, the finished block can be
seen in diagram b. Refer to the quilt assembly
diagram for fabric placement. Piece the
blocks together into 3 rows of 6 blocks using
the Template MM and NN triangles to set
the blocks 'on point' as shown in the quilt
assembly diagram.

MAKING THE QUILT

Lay out the pieced columns and sashing
strips with the narrow sashing strips between
the pieced columns and the wide sashing
strips on the outer edges of the quilt as
shown in the quilt assembly diagram. Trim the
sashing strips to fit exactly and join the
pieced columns and sashing strips together.

FINISHING THE QUILT

Press the quilt top. Seam the backing pieces
using a ¼in (6mm) seam allowance to form a
piece approx. 93in x 83in (236cm x 211cm).
Layer the quilt top, batting and backing and
baste together (see page 122). Using ochre
machine quilting thread, quilt in the ditch
around the blocks and in the sashing seams,
then free style quilt around the flowers in
the sashing strips. In the template MM and
NN shapes quilt lines offset 1½in (3.75cm)
from the block seams. Trim the quilt edges
and attach the binding (see page 122).

Block Assembly Diagrams

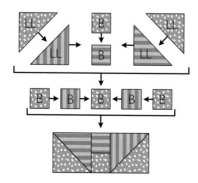

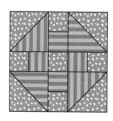

b

a

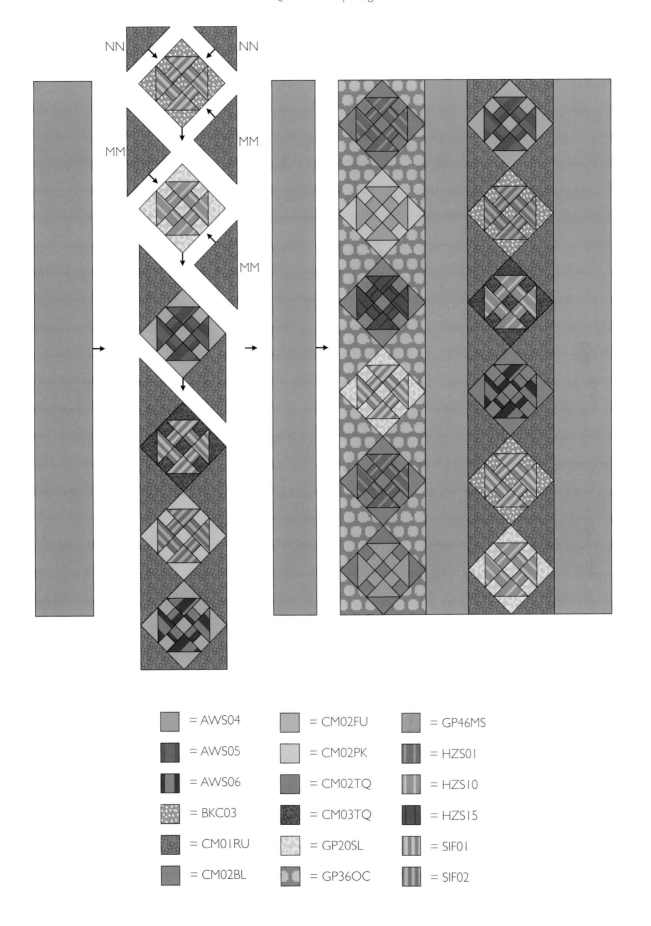

= AWS04	= CM02FU	= GP46MS	
= AWS05	= CM02PK	= HZS01	
= AWS06	= CM02TQ	= HZS10	
= BKC03	= CM03TQ	= HZS15	
= CM01RU	= GP20SL	= SIF01	
= CM02BL	= GP36OC	= SIF02	

Morning Garden Quilt ★★

Kaffe Fassett

With the same layout as Tapestry Garden I've used a high pastel palette. Martha Negley fruit & floral prints were so delicious to arrange. Elegant colour tones create such an old world harmony with a modern freshness.

SIZE OF QUILT
The finished quilt will measure approx.
95in × 62in (241.5cm × 157.5cm).

MATERIALS
Patchwork Fabrics:
BAS-RELIEF
Peach   DW01PH: ½ yd (45cm)
FOLIAGE
Aqua   DW02AQ: ½ yd (45cm)
Ochre   DW02OC: ½ yd (45cm)
RENAISSANCE LEAF
Sky Blue   DW05SK: ½ yd (45cm)
HARVEST TOILE
Fuchsia   GP35FU: ⅜ yd (35cm)
Lilac   GP35LI: ⅜ yd (35cm)
Teal   GP35TE: ⅝ yd (60cm)
CABBAGE & ROSES
Spring   GP38SP: ⅝ yd (60cm)
EMBROIDERED LEAF
Pink   GP42PK: ⅝ yd (60cm)
PUFF
Multi   GP43MU: ¼ yd (25cm)
LILIES
Lime   GP45LM: ½ yd (45cm)
CLOISONNE
Aqua   GP46AQ: ⅝ yd (60cm)
DOTTED LEAF
Pink   LC03PK: ¼ yd (25cm)
NOSEGAY
Fuchsia   LC04FU: ⅜ yd (35cm)
ARBOUR
Duck Egg   LC05DE: ½ yd (45cm)
Green   LC05GN: ¼ yd (25cm)
Pink   LC05PK: ¼ yd (25cm)
Borders:
FOLIAGE
Grey   DW02GY: 2½ yds (2.3m)

Backing Fabric: 6 yds (5.5m)
We suggest these fabrics for backing:
FOLIAGE, Aqua DW02AQ, Grey DW02GY.
LILIES, Lime GP45LM

Binding:
ARBOUR
Duck Egg   LC05DE: ¾ yd (70cm)

Batting:
103in × 70in (261.5cm × 178cm).

Quilting thread:
Toning machine quilting thread.

Templates:
see pages 110, 111

AA   W   Large Square

PATCH SHAPES
This quilt is made using 1 small square patch shape (Template AA), 1 medium square (Template W) and 1 large square, cut to size. The Squares are pieced into 3 columns which are then joined to form the quilt centre. The quilt is finished with a border with corner posts.

CUTTING OUT
To reduce waste cut the large patch shapes

first, reserve the remaining strips and trim for smaller patch shapes.

Large Square: Cut 9½in (24.25cm) wide strips across the width of the fabric. Each strip will give you 4 patches per 45in (114cm) wide fabric. From the strips cut 9½in (24.25cm) squares. Cut 4 in GP35TE, 3 in GP38SP, GP42PK, GP46AQ, 2 in DW02AQ, 1 in DW01PH, DW02OC, DW05SK, GP35FU, GP45LM and LC05DE.

Template W: Cut 6½in (16.5cm) wide strips across the width of the fabric. Each strip will give you 6 patches per 45in (114cm) wide fabric. Cut 6 in GP38SP, 5 in GP35FU, GP35LI, GP35TE, 4 in DW02OC, LC05DE, 3 in DW01PH, DW02AQ, DW05SK, GP46AQ, LC05PK, 2 in GP45LM, LC03PK, LC04FU, 1 in GP42PK and LC05GN.

Template AA: Cut 3½in (9cm) wide strips across the width of the fabric. Each strip will give you 12 patches per 45in (114cm) wide fabric. Cut 13 in GP43MU, 12 in DW02OC, 11 in GP35LI, 10 in LC04FU, 9 in DW02AQ, GP46AQ, LC05DE, 8 in LC05GN, 7 in DW01PH, 6 in DW05SK, GP35TE, GP38SP, 5 in GP42PK, GP45LM, LC03PK and 4 in LC05PK.

Borders: Along the length of the fabric cut 2 strips 87½in × 4½in (222.25cm × 11.5cm) and 2 strips 54½in × 4½in (138.5cm × 11.5cm) in DW02GY.

Corner Posts: Cut 4 × 4½in (11.5cm) squares in GP42PK.

Binding: Cut 8 strips 2½in (6.5cm) wide × width of fabric in LC05DE.

Backing: Cut 1 piece 42in × 103in (106.5cm × 261.5cm) and 1 piece 28½in × 103in (72.5cm × 261.5cm) in backing fabric.

MAKING THE QUILT

Use a ¼in (6mm) seam allowance throughout. Lay out the patches for the left column, separate them into horizontal rows, Piece the rows, sub-piecing the smaller sections as you go. Refer to the quilt assembly diagram for fabric placement and guidance. Repeat in the same manner for the middle and right columns. Join the columns to form the quilt centre. Join the top and bottom borders to the quilt centre. Join a corner post to the ends of each side border and then join the side borders to the quilt centre as shown in the quilt assembly diagram.

FINISHING THE QUILT

Press the quilt top. Seam the backing pieces using a ¼in (6mm) seam allowance to form a piece approx. 103in × 70in (261.5cm × 178cm). Layer the quilt top, batting and backing and baste together (see page 122). Using toning quilting thread, quilt diagonally in both directions across each square, or if you prefer quilt in the ditch around the patch shapes. Trim the quilt edges and attach the binding (see page 122).

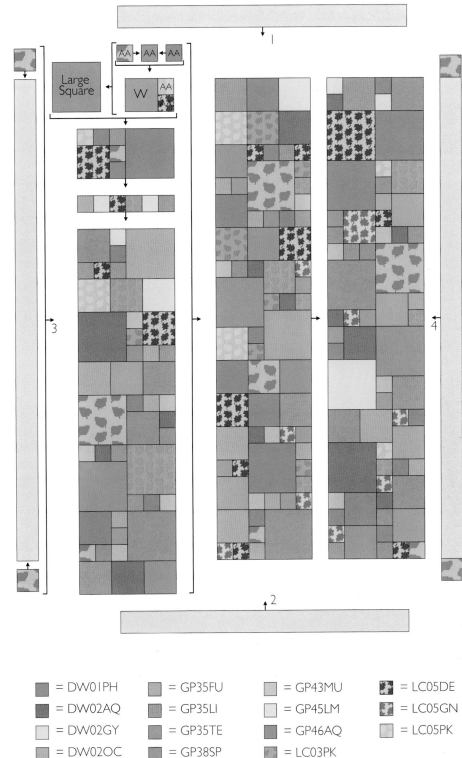

= DW01PH	= GP35FU	= GP43MU	= LC05DE
= DW02AQ	= GP35LI	= GP45LM	= LC05GN
= DW02GY	= GP35TE	= GP46AQ	= LC05PK
= DW02OC	= GP38SP	= LC03PK	
= DW05SK	= GP42PK	= LC04FU	

Tapestry Garden Quilt ★

KAFFE FASSETT

In my book, 'Passionate Patchwork', I did a quilt using all shirt stripings arranged in three different scale squares. I felt the same layout in Leafy Florals would be good. I've used a lot of David Wolverson classic prints in their deep mysterious colour tones.

SIZE OF QUILT
The finished quilt will measure approx.
95in × 62in (241.5cm × 157.5cm).

MATERIALS
Patchwork Fabrics:
BAS-RELIEF
Green   DW01GN: ⅝ yd (60cm)
Purple   DW01PU: ½ yd (45cm)
MEDIEVAL ROSE
Leafy   DW04LF: ½ yd (45cm)
RENAISSANCE LEAF
Brown   DW05BR: ½ yd (45cm)
Purple   DW05PU: ½ yd (45cm)
HARVEST TOILE
Jade   GP35JA: ⅝ yd (60cm)
EMBROIDERED LEAF
Plum   GP42PL: ½ yd (45cm)
PUFF
Green   GP43GN: ¼ yd (25cm)
LILIES
Malachite   GP45MA: ⅝ yd (60cm)
CLOISONNE
Aqua   GP46AQ: ¼ yd (25cm)
Teal   GP46TE: ½ yd (45cm) or
               use leftover from borders.
BURNTWOOD ROSE
Teal   GP47TE: ⅜ yd (35cm)
VEGETABLE DOT
Dark   MN02DK: ¼ yd (25cm)
Natural   MN02NL: ⅜ yd (35cm)
TWIG STRIPE
Dark   MN03DK: ⅛ yd (15cm)
VEGETABLE STRIPE
Dark   MN04DK: ½ yd (45cm)
VEGETABLE LEAVES
Dark   MN05DK: ½ yd (45cm)
Natural   MN05NL: ½ yd (45cm)
DOTTED LEAF
Green   LC03GN: ⅜ yd (35cm)
Borders:
CLOISONNE
Teal   GP46TE: 2½ yd (2.3m)

Backing Fabric: 6 yds (5.5m)
We suggest these fabrics for backing:
CLOISONNE, Teal GP46TE
VEGETABLE DOT, Dark MN02DK

Binding:
VEGETABLE LEAVES
Dark   MN05DK: ¾ yd (70cm)

Batting:
103in × 70in (261.5cm × 178cm).

Quilting thread:
Toning machine quilting thread.

Templates:
See Morning Garden Quilt

PATCH SHAPES
See Morning Garden Quilt

CUTTING OUT
To reduce waste cut the large patch shapes
first, reserve the remaining strips and trim for
smaller patch shapes.
Large Square: Cut 9½in (24.25cm) wide
strips across the width of the fabric. Each
strip will give you 4 patches per 45in
(114cm) wide fabric. From the strips cut
9½in (24.25cm) squares. Cut 4 in GP45MA,
3 in GP35JA, 2 in DW05BR, MN05DK, 1 in
DW01GN, DW01PU, DW04LF, DW05PU,
GP42PL, GP46TE, GP47TE, MN04DK and
MN05NL.
Template W: Cut 6½in (16.5cm) wide strips
across the width of the fabric. Each strip will
give you 6 patches per 45in (114cm) wide
fabric. Cut 7 in GP35JA, 5 in GP45MA,
GP46TE, 4 in DW01GN, 3 in DW01PU,
DW04LF, DW05PU, GP42PL, MN02NL,
MN04DK, MN05NL, LC03GN, 2 in
DW05BR, GP47TE, MN02DK, 1 in GP46AQ
and MN05DK.
Template AA: Cut 3½in (9cm) wide strips
across the width of the fabric. Each strip will
give you 12 patches per 45in (114cm) wide
fabric. Cut 15 in GP43GN, 11 in GP35JA, 9 in
DW01PU, MN04DK, 8 in DW01GN, GP42PL,
MN02NL, LC03GN, 7 in GP45MA, 6 in
GP46AQ, MN05DK, 5 in DW04LF, GP46TE,
MN03DK, MN05NL, 4 in DW05BR, DW05PU,
GP47TE and 3 in MN02DK.
Borders: Along the length of the fabric cut 2
strips 87½in x 4½in (222.25cm x11.5cm) and
2 strips 54½in x 4½in (138.5cm x 11.5cm) in
GP46TE.
Corner Posts: Cut 4 x 4½in (11.5cm)
squares in DW01GN.

Binding: Cut 8 strips 2½in (6.5cm) wide x
width of fabric in MN05DK.

Backing: Cut 1 piece 42in x 103in (106.5cm
x 261.5cm) and 1 piece 28½in x 103in
(72.5cm x 261.5cm) in backing fabric.

MAKING THE QUILT
See Morning Garden Quilt instructions.

FINISHING THE QUILT
See Morning Garden Quilt instructions.

Quilt Assembly Diagram

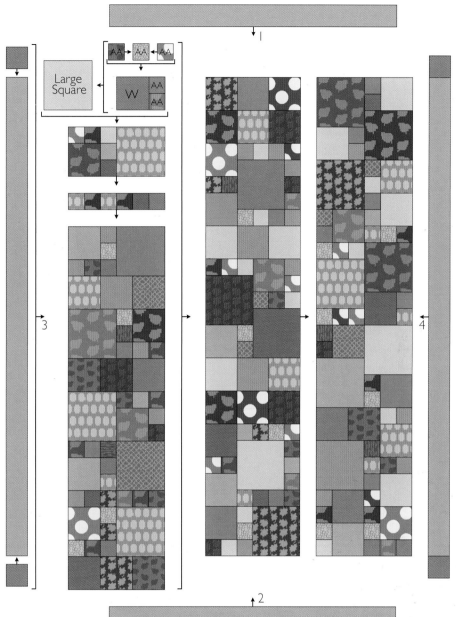

▦ = DW01PU		▧ = GP47TE
▦ = DW04LF		◣ = MN02DK
▦ = DW05BR		◩ = MN02NL
▦ = DW05PU		▦ = MN03DK
▦ = GP35JA		▦ = MN04DK
▦ = GP42PL		▦ = MN05DK
▦ = GP43GN		▦ = MN05NL
▦ = GP45MA		▦ = LC03GN
▦ = GP46AQ		
▦ = GP46TE		

Matisse Villa Quilt ★★

ROBERTA HORTON

Matisse's father and grandfather were weavers. No wonder he grew up loving fabric, just as we do. His paintings featuring textiles are filled with flowers and stripes and lots of colour. Ah, the opportunity to translate this thought into a quilt!

We suggest these fabrics for backing: FLOWER BASKET, Magenta GP48MG or Black GP48BK.
Note: Extra fabric has been allowed for pattern matching.

Binding:
WOVEN HAZE STRIPE
Purple   HZS14: ¾ yd (70cm)

Batting:
80in × 80in (203cm × 203cm).

Quilting thread:
Invisible, red and yellow machine quilting thread.

Templates:
see pages 107, 110, 111

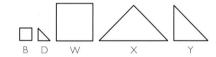

PATCH SHAPES
Blocks made using 2 square patch shapes (Templates B & W) and 1 triangle patch shape (Template D) are set 'on point' into rows using 2 triangle patch shapes (Templates X and Y). You'll find half template X on page 111. Take a large piece of paper, fold, place the edge of template X to the fold of paper, trace around shape and cut out. Open out for the complete template. The pieced rows are interspaced with sashing strips and then surrounded with a simple inner border. The quilt is then finished with an outer border with corner posts (Template W).

CUTTING OUT
Template B: Cut 2½in (6.5cm) wide strips across the width of the fabric. Each strip will give you 16 patches per 45in (114cm) wide fabric. Cut 20 in LC03GN.
Template D: Cut 2⅞in (7.25cm) wide strips across the width of the fabric. Each strip will give you 28 patches per 45in (114cm) wide fabric. Cut 120 in LC03GN, 60 in GP01PU and GP44BL.
Template W: Cut 6½in (16.5cm) wide strips across the width of the fabric. Each strip will give you 6 patches per 45in (114cm) wide fabric. Cut 10 in GP42VI and GP43RD. Also

SIZE OF QUILT
The finished quilt will measure approx. 73¼in × 72½in (186cm × 184cm).

MATERIALS
Patchwork Fabrics:
ROMAN GLASS
Purple   GP01PU: ⅜ yd (35cm)
SPOOLS
Magenta   GP34MG: ¼ yd (25cm)
CABBAGE & ROSES
Wood   GP38WD: 1⅝ yds (1.5m)
ROMANY
Jewel   GP39JW: 1¼ yds (1.15m)

EMBROIDERED LEAF
Violet   GP42VI: ½ yd (45cm)
PUFF
Red   GP43RD: ½ yd (45cm)
CAMOUFLAGE
Blue   GP44BL: ⅜ yd (35cm)
FLOWER BASKET
Black   GP48BK: ⅝ yd (60cm)
HYDRANGEA
Black   LC02BK: ½ yd (45cm)
DOTTED LEAVES
Green   LC03GN: ⅝ yd (60cm)

Backing Fabric: 5 yds (4.6m)

Cut 4 in GP34MG for outer border sashing posts.

Template X: Cut 12½in (31.75cm) wide strips across the width of the fabric in GP38WD. Each strip will give you 12 patches per 45in (114cm) wide fabric. Cut 8 x 12½in (31.75cm) squares, then using the template as a guide cut each square twice diagonally to make 4 triangles. This will ensure the long side of the triangle will not have a bias edge. Cut 32 in GP38WD.

Template Y: Cut 6½in (16.5cm) wide strips across the width of the fabric. Each strip will give you 12 patches per 45in (114cm) wide fabric. Cut 16 in GP38WD.

Sashing: Cut 4 strips 4½in (11.5cm) wide x width of fabric in GP48BK. Join strips as necessary and cut 3 sashing strips 57in x 4½in (144.75cm x 11.5cm).

Inner Border: Cut 6 strips 2½in (6.5cm) wide x width of fabric in LC02BK. Join strips as necessary and cut 2 strips 61¾in x 2½in (157cm x 6.5cm) for the side inner borders and 2 strips 57in x 2½in (144.75cm x 6.5cm) for the top and bottom inner borders.

Outer Border: Cut 6 strips 6½in (16.5cm) wide x width of fabric in GP39JW. Join strips as necessary and cut 2 strips 61¾in x 6½in (157cm x 16.5cm) and 2 strips 61in x 6½in (155cm x 16.5cm).

Binding: Cut 8¼yds (7.5m) of 2½in (6.5cm) wide bias binding in HZS14.

Backing: Cut 2 pieces 41in x 80in (104cm x 203cm) in backing fabric. A generous amount of fabric has been allowed so that the large pattern can be matched.

MAKING THE BLOCKS AND ROWS
Use a ¼in (6mm) seam allowance throughout. Piece 20 blocks following block assembly diagrams a, b and c. There are 2 colourways for the blocks, make 10 of each referring to the quilt assembly diagram for fabric placement. Piece the blocks together into 4 rows of 5 blocks using the Template X and Y triangles to set the blocks 'on point' as shown in the row assembly diagram.

MAKING THE QUILT
Interspace the pieced rows with sashing strips as shown in the quilt assembly diagram. Join the top and bottom, then side inner borders to the quilt centre. Join the side outer borders to the quilt centre, join a corner post to each end of the top and bottom outer borders and join to the quilt centre.

Block Assembly Diagrams

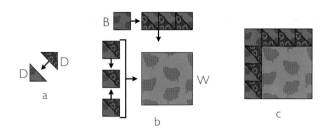

Row Assembly Diagram

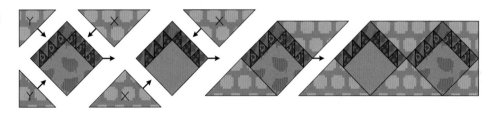

Quilting Diagram

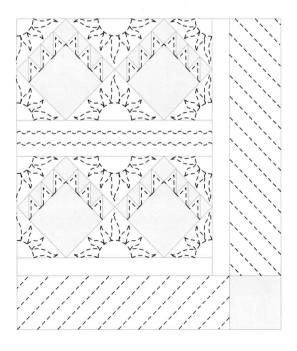

FINISHING THE QUILT

Press the quilt top. Seam the backing pieces using a ¼in (6mm) seam allowance to form a piece approx. 80in x 80in (203cm x 203cm). Layer the quilt top, batting and backing and baste together (see page 122). Using invisible machine quilting thread, quilt in the ditch in the block, sashing, inner and outer border seams. As shown in the quilting diagram using red quilting thread meander quilt the grey coloured areas, quilt parallel squiggly lines in the sashing and diagonal lines in the outer border following the fabric print. In yellow quilting thread quilt ½ sun shapes in the template X patch shapes and ¼ sun shapes in the template Y patch shapes adding freeform rays. Trim the quilt edges and attach the binding (see page 122).

Quilt Assembly Diagram

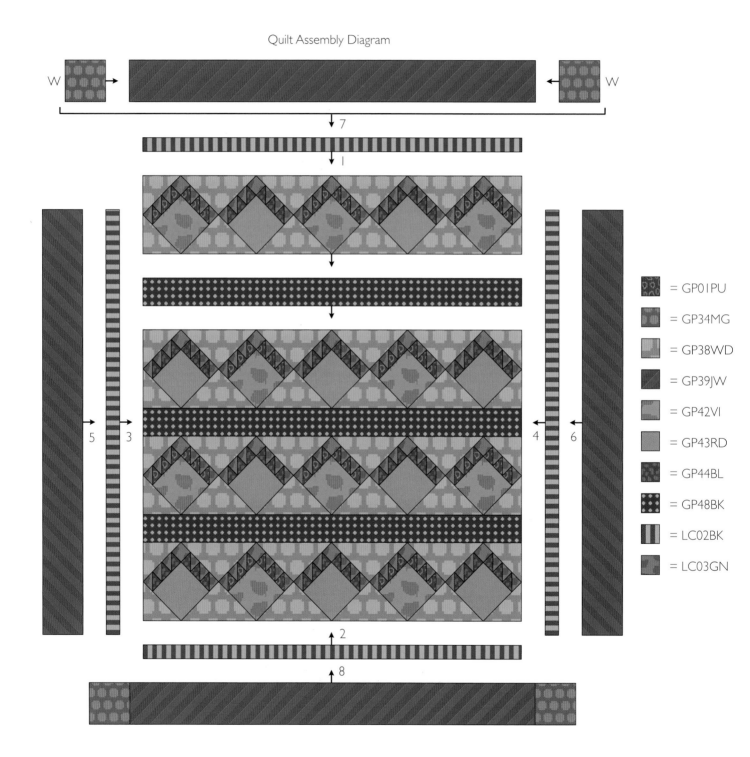

= GP01PU

= GP34MG

= GP38WD

= GP39JW

= GP42VI

= GP43RD

= GP44BL

= GP48BK

= LC02BK

= LC03GN

66

Rustic Snowballs Quilt ★

BRANDON MABLY

This quilt was inspired by the post card of a Vintage Snowball that I found on my travels. I love the scrappy quality of the fabrics which look like some one used hand-me-down cloths cut up. I tried to arrive at the same mood using the Kaffe Fassett range here.

SIZE OF QUILT
The finished quilt will measure approx. 76½in x 58½in (194.5cm x 148.5cm).

MATERIALS
Patchwork Fabrics:
AWNING STRIPE
Duck Egg   AWS03: ½ yd (45cm)
LAVA
Rust   CM01RU: ⅜ yd (35cm)
MARBLE
Fuchsia   CM02FU: ¼ yd (25cm)
CHICKEN SCRATCH
Fuchsia   CM05FU: ½ yd (45cm)
Turquoise   CM05TQ: ⅝ yd (60cm)
EXOTIC STRIPE
                 ES10: ½ yd (45cm)
PAPERWEIGHT
Gypsy   GP20GY: ⅜ yd (35cm)
FRECKLES
Moss   GP40MS: ½ yd (45cm)
PLANETS
Marquetry   GP41MQ: ⅜ yd (35cm)
PUFF
Antique   GP43AN: ⅜ yd (35cm)
Brown   GP43BR: ⅜ yd (35cm)
CAMOUFLAGE
Black   GP44BK: ⅜ yd (35cm)
ISLANDS
Gold   GP49GD: ⅞ yd (80cm)
WOVEN HAZE STRIPE
Blush   HZS09: ¼ yd (25cm)
FLOWER SPRAYS
Black   LC01BK: ⅝ yd (60cm)
Gold   LC01GD: ⅜ yd (35cm)
HYDRANGEA
Tobacco   LC02TO: ⅜ yd (35cm)
ARBOUR
Tobacco   LC05TO: ½ yd (45cm)
TWIG STRIPE
Dark   MN03DK: ½ yd (45cm)

Backing Fabric: 3¾ yds (3.5m)
We suggest these fabrics for backing:

ORGANIC DOTS, Brown GP53BR
PUFF, Brown GP43BR
PLANETS, Marquetry GP41MQ

Binding:
ARBOUR
Tobacco   LC05TO: ⅝ yd (60cm)

Batting:
84in x 66in (213cm x 167.5cm).

Quilting thread:
Caramel hand quilting thread.

Templates:
see pages 108, 116

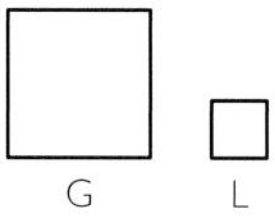

PATCH SHAPES
This quilt is pieced from a traditional Snowball block, made from an octagon and four triangles, in this case it is made 'the easy way' by using a large square (Template G) and 4 small squares (Template L) for each block. The small squares are placed over the corners of the large squares and stitched diagonally. They are then trimmed and flipped back to replace the corners of the large square.

CUTTING OUT
Template G: Cut 5in (12.75cm) wide strips across the width of the fabric. Each strip will give you 8 patches per 45in (114cm) wide fabric. Cut 25 in LC01BK, 21 in ES10, 20 in AWS03, LC05TO, 19 in MN03DK, 14 in CM01RU, GP20GY, 13 in GP43AN, GP43BR, GP44BK, LC01GD, 12 in GP41MQ, LC02TO, 6 in CM02FU and HZS09.
Template L: Cut 1¾in (4.5cm) wide strips across the width of the fabric. Each strip will give you 24 patches per 45in (114cm) wide

fabric. Cut 364 in GP49GD, 208 in CM05TQ, 156 in CM05FU and GP40MS.

Binding: cut 7 strips 2½in (6.5cm) wide x width of fabric in LC05TO.

Backing: Cut 2 pieces 66in x 42½in (167.5cm by 108cm) in backing fabric.

MAKING THE BLOCKS
To make the Snowball blocks take one large square (template G) and four small squares (template L), using the quilt assembly diagram as a guide to fabric combinations. Place one small square, right sides together onto each corner of the large square, matching the edges carefully as shown in block assembly diagram a. Stitch diagonally across the small squares as shown in diagram b. Trim the corners to a ¼in (6mm) seam allowance and press the corners out (diagram c). Make 221 blocks. Note: The ISLANDS fabric used for some of the corners of the snowball blocks has 2 separate design elements. Separate the yellow and orange squares into 2 piles and use as if they are 2 fabrics so that when the blocks are joined to form the quilt the 'squares' in each horizontal row appear to be a single colour.

MAKING THE QUILT
Join the blocks into 17 rows of 13 blocks as shown in the quilt assembly diagram. Join the rows to form the quilt.

FINISHING THE QUILT
Press the quilt top. Seam the backing pieces using a ¼in (6mm) seam allowance to form a piece approx. 84in x 66in (213cm x 167.5cm). Layer the quilt top, batting and backing and baste together (see page 122). Using caramel hand quilting thread, quilt a 3in (7.75cm) diameter circle in the centre of each block. Trim the quilt edges and attach the binding (see page 122).

Block Assembly Diagrams

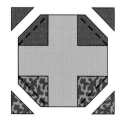

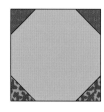

a   b   c

Quilt Assembly Diagram

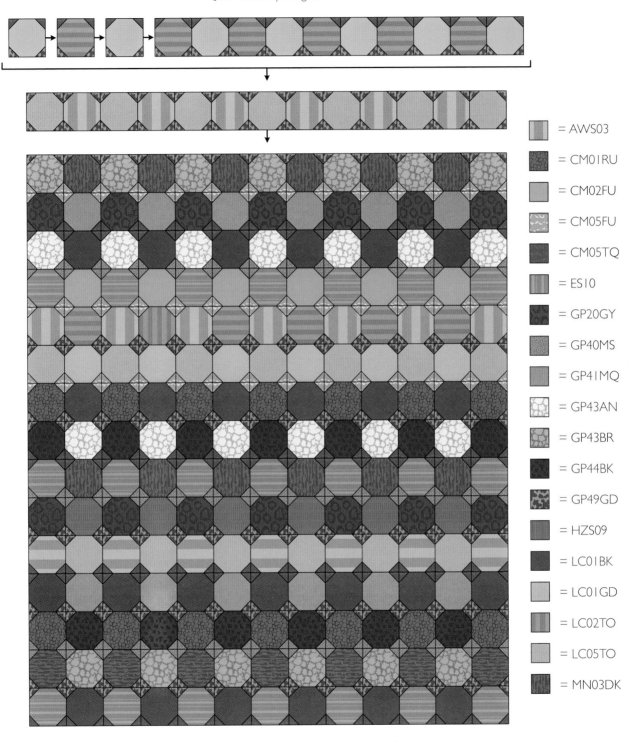

	= AWS03
	= CM01RU
	= CM02FU
	= CM05FU
	= CM05TQ
	= ES10
	= GP20GY
	= GP40MS
	= GP41MQ
	= GP43AN
	= GP43BR
	= GP44BK
	= GP49GD
	= HZS09
	= LC01BK
	= LC01GD
	= LC02TO
	= LC05TO
	= MN03DK

Cabin Fever Quilt ★★

KAFFE FASSETT

The old school house block has always fascinated me. Instead of doing it in solids which is more usual, I used florals and textures to give it movement and intrigue. There is a light and dark element as well.

SIZE OF QUILT
The finished quilt will measure approx. 73in x 61in (185.5cm x 155cm).

MATERIALS
Patchwork Fabrics:
MARBLE
Fuchsia   CM02FU: ⅜ yd (35cm)
CHICKEN SCRATCH
Black   CM05BK: ⅝ yd (60cm)
Pink   CM05PK: ⅝ yd (60cm)

ROMAN GLASS
Byzantium   GP01BY: ⅜ yd (35cm)
PUFF
Brown   GP43BR: ⅜ yd (35cm)
Peat   GP43PA: ⅜ yd (35cm)
CAMOUFLAGE
Black   GP44BK: ⅜ yd (35cm)
Green   GP44GN: ⅜ yd (35cm)
LILIES
Wood   GP45WD: ⅜ yd (35cm)

BURNT WOOD ROSE
Midnight   GP47MD: ⅜ yd (35cm)
FLOWER BASKET
Black   GP48BK: ⅜ yd (35cm)
ISLANDS
Bottle   GP49BT: ⅜ yd (35cm)
Moss   GP49MS: 1⅞ yds (1.7m)
                   incl borders.

Sashing:
CHICKEN SCRATCH
Rust   CM05RU: 1¼ yds (1.15m)

Borders:
ISLANDS
Moss   GP49MS:
                   see patchwork fabrics.

Backing Fabric: 4 yds (3.7m)
We suggest these fabrics for backing:
PUFF, Peat GP43PA
BURNT WOOD ROSE, Midnight GP47MD

Binding:
CAMOUFLAGE
Black   GP44BK:
                   see patchwork fabrics

Batting:
81in x 69in (206cm x 175cm).

Quilting thread:
Toning machine quilting thread.

Templates:
see pages 107, 108, 109

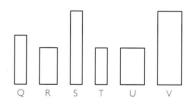

PATCH SHAPES
The cabin blocks (finish 10in/25.5cm) are made using 1 square patch shape (Template B), 1 triangle patch shape (Template D) and 9 rectangle patch shapes (Templates N, O, P,

Template Position Diagram

Block Assembly Diagram

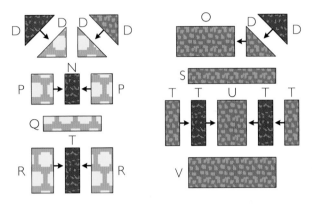

a

Q, R, S, T, U, & V). Refer to the diagram (above) for template position details. The blocks are separated and surrounded with sashing strips cut to size. The quilt is then finished with a simple border.

CUTTING OUT

Borders: Along the length of the fabric cut 2 strips 6in x 62½in x (15.25cm x 158.75cm) and 2 strips 6in x 61½in x (15.25cm x 156.25cm) in GP49MS. Reserve remaining fabric for cutting block template shapes.

Template D: Cut 2⅞in (7.25cm) wide strips across the width of the fabric. Cut 20 in CM05BK, CM05PK, 10 in GP44GN, 8 in GP43BR, GP44BK, GP45WD, GP49BT, GP49MS, 6 in CM02FU, GP01BY, GP43PA, GP47MD and GP48BK. Trim leftover strips for other templates.

Template B: Cut 2½ in (6.5cm) wide strips across the width of the fabric. Each strip will give you 16 patches per 45in (114cm) wide fabric. Cut 20 in CM05BK and CM05PK.

Template O: Cut 2½ in (6.5cm) wide strips across the width of the fabric. Each strip will give you 9 patches per 45in (114cm) wide fabric. Cut 10 in CM05BK, CM05PK, 3 in GP45WD, 2 in CM02FU, GP43PA, GP44BK, GP44GN, GP47MD, GP48BK, GP49MS, 1 in GP01BY, GP43BR and GP49BT.

Template U: Cut 2½ in (6.5cm) wide strips across the width of the fabric. Cut 3 in GP45WD, 2 in CM02FU, GP43PA, GP44BK, GP44GN, GP47MD, GP48BK, GP49MS, 1 in GP01BY, GP43BR and GP49BT.

Template V: Cut 2½ in (6.5cm) wide strips across the width of the fabric. Cut 3 in GP45WD, 2 in CM02FU, GP43PA, GP44BK, GP44GN, GP47MD, GP48BK, GP49MS, 1 in GP01BY, GP43BR and GP49BT.

Template P: Cut 2in (5cm) wide strips across the width of the fabric. Cut 6 in GP43BR, GP44GN, GP49BT, 4 in GP01BY, GP44BK, GP49MS, 2 in CM02FU, GP43PA, GP45WD, GP47MD and GP48BK.

Template R: Cut 2in (5cm) wide strips across the width of the fabric, Cut 6 in GP43BR, GP44GN, GP49BT, 4 in GP01BY, GP44BK, GP49MS, 2 in CM02FU, GP43PA, GP45WD, GP47MD and GP48BK.

Template N: Cut 1½in (3.75cm) wide strips across the width of the fabric. Each strip will give you 16 patches per 45in (114cm) wide fabric. Cut 10 in CM05BK, CM05PK, 6 in GP45WD, 4 in CM02FU, GP43PA, GP44BK, GP44GN, GP47MD, GP48BK, GP49MS, 2 in GP01BY, GP43BR and GP49BT.

Template Q: Cut 1½in (3.75cm) wide strips across the width of the fabric. Cut 3 in GP43BR, GP44GN, GP49BT, 2 in GP01BY, GP44BK, GP49MS, 1 in CM02FU, GP43PA, GP45WD, GP47MD and GP48BK.

Template S: Cut 1½in (3.75cm) wide strips across the width of the fabric. Cut 3 in GP45WD, 2 in CM02FU, GP43PA, GP44BK,

Block Assembly Diagrams

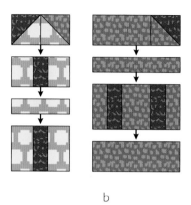

b

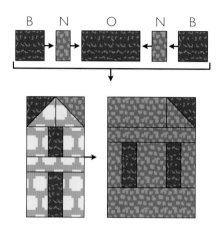

B   N   O   N   B

c

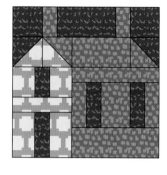

d

GP44GN, GP47MD, GP48BK, GP49MS, 1 in GP01BY, GP43BR and GP49BT.
Template T: Cut 1½in (3.75cm) wide strips across the width of the fabric. Cut 30 in CM05BK, CM05PK, 6 in GP45WD, 4 in CM02FU, GP43PA, GP44BK, GP44GN, GP47MD, GP48BK, GP49MS, 2 in GP01BY, GP43BR and GP49BT.

Sashing: Cut 14 strips 2½in (6.5cm) wide × width of fabric in CM05RU. Join strips as necessary then cut 2 strips 2½in × 58½in (6.5cm × 148.5cm), 2 strips 2½in × 50½in (6.5cm × 128.25cm), 4 strips 2½in × 46½in (6.5cm × 118cm) and 15 strips 2½in × 10½in (6.5cm × 26.75cm).

Binding: Cut 7 strips 2½in (6.5cm) wide × width of fabric in GP44BK.

Backing: Cut 2 pieces 41in × 69in (104cm × 175cm) in backing fabric.

MAKING THE BLOCKS
Use a ¼in (6mm) seam allowance throughout. Referring to the quilt assembly diagram for fabric placement piece 20 cabin blocks following block assembly diagrams a, b and c, the finished block can be seen in diagram d.

MAKING THE QUILT
Lay the blocks out as shown in the quilt assembly diagram. Join the blocks into 5 rows of 4 blocks, interspacing the blocks with the short sashing strips. Join the 5 rows interspacing the rows with the 2½in × 46½in (6.5cm × 118cm) sashing strips. Next join the 2½in × 58½in (6.5cm × 148.5cm) sashing strips to the quilt sides and then the 2½in ×

50½in (6.5cm × 128.25cm) sashing strips to the top and bottom. Finally join the border in the order indicated in the quilt assembly diagram.

FINISHING THE QUILT
Press the quilt top. Seam the backing pieces using a ¼in (6mm) seam allowance to form a piece approx. 81in × 69in (206cm × 175cm). Layer the quilt top, batting and backing and baste together (see page 122). Using a toning machine quilting thread, quilt in the ditch in the block and sashing seams. Quilt the outer border with 4 parallel lines spaced ½in (1.25cm) apart from the inner seam, then 2 more lines spaced ½in (1.25cm) apart from outer edge of the quilt. Trim the quilt edges and attach the binding (see page 122).

Quilt Assembly Diagram

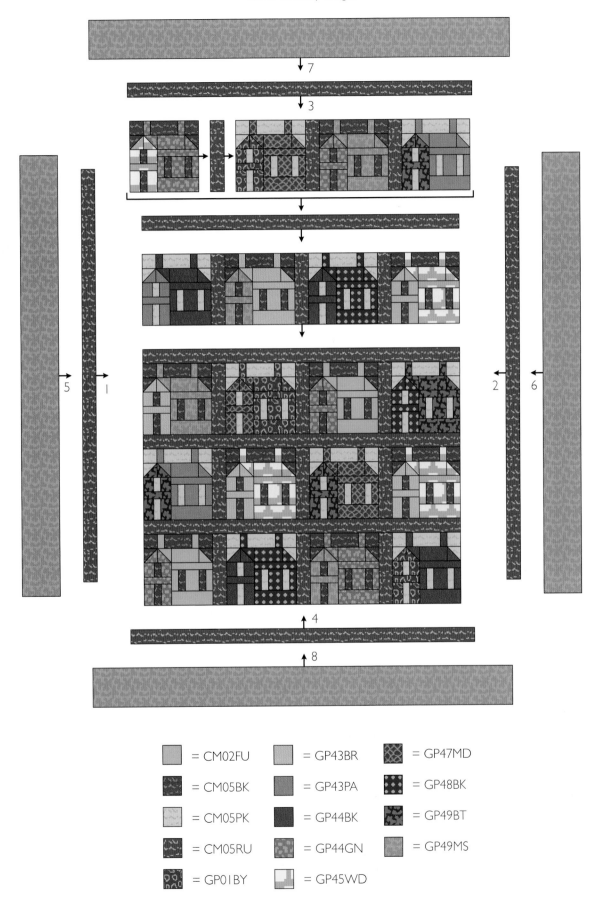

= CM02FU	= GP43BR	= GP47MD
= CM05BK	= GP43PA	= GP48BK
= CM05PK	= GP44BK	= GP49BT
= CM05RU	= GP44GN	= GP49MS
= GP01BY	= GP45WD	

Little Boxes Quilt ★★

PAULINE SMITH

Rows of terraced houses in rich blue and red stripes and florals make a simple cot quilt.

SIZE OF QUILT
The finished quilt will measure approx. 38½in × 36in (98cm × 91.5cm).

MATERIALS
Patchwork Fabrics:
PAPERWEIGHT
Paprika   GP20PP: ¼ yd (25cm)
BEAD STRIPE
Cobalt   GP50CB: ¼ yd (25cm)
Magenta   GP50MG: ¼ yd (25cm)
SHIRT STRIPES
Midnight   GP51MD: ¼ yd (25cm)
Red   GP51RD: ⅜ yd (35cm)
AURICULA
Red   GP52RD: ⅜ yd (35cm)
ORGANIC DOTS
Midnight   GP53MD: ¼ yd (25cm)

HAZE STRIPE
Persimmon   HZS01: ¼ yd (25cm)
Mustard   HZS02: ¼ yd (25cm)
Navy   HZS13: ⅜ yd (35cm)
SHOT COTTON
Forget-me-not SC51: ⅛ yd (15cm)
Brick   SC58: ⅛ yd (15cm)

Backing Fabric: 1⅜ yds (1.25m)
We suggest these fabrics for backing:
AURICULA, Red GP52RD or
Indigo GP52IN

Binding:
HAZE STRIPE
Fuchsia   HZS07: ⅜ yd (35cm)

Batting:
46in × 44in (117cm × 112cm).

Quilting thread:
Toning machine quilting thread.

Templates:
see pages 111, 112, 113

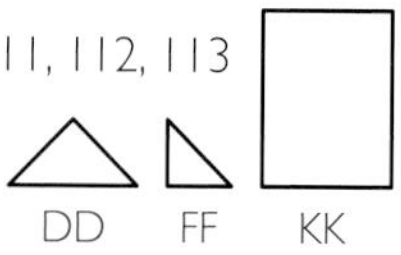

DD FF KK

PATCH SHAPES
2 triangle patch shapes (Templates DD & FF) are pieced into rows to form the roofs of the little houses. The houses are pieced using 1 rectangle patch shape (Template KK), which are joined into rows and alternated with the roof rows. Some of the houses have 'windows' appliquéd.

CUTTING OUT
The stripe directions are important in this quilt, so please read the cutting instructions carefully and refer to the diagram for additional help.

Template DD: Fabric HZS02, cut 1 × 6⅜ in (16.25cm) wide strip across the width of the fabric. Refer to the cutting diagram for fabric HZS02, cut 33 patch shapes as shown, this will ensure the stripe direction runs correctly. Fabrics GP53MD, HZS01, HZS13, SC12 and SC14, cut 2⅛ in (5.5cm) wide strips across the width of the fabric. Each strip will give you 19 patches per 45in (114cm) wide fabric. Place the template with the long side along the cut edge of the strip. Cut 44 in HZS13, 33 in GP53MD, 25 in HZS01, 14 in SC58 and 12 in SC51.
Template FF: Cut 2⅜in (6cm) wide strips across the width of the fabric. Cut 8 in HZS13 and 6 in GP53MD.
Template KK: Fabrics GP20PP and GP52RD, cut 4½in (11.5cm) wide strips across the width of the fabric. Each strip will give you 12 patches per 45in (114cm) wide fabric. Cut 20 in GP52RD and 7 in GP20PP. Fabrics GP50CB, GP50MG, GP51MD and GP51RD have a stripe pattern in the prints. To get the correct stripe directions cut as follows. For each of these fabrics cut 1 × 4½ in (11.5cm) wide strips across the width of the fabric. Each strip will give you 12 patches per 45in (114cm) wide fabric. Cut 9 in GP51MD, GP51RD, 7 in GP50CB and 6 in GP50MG. Next Cut 3½in (9cm) wide strips across the width of the fabric. Each strip will

Quilt Assembly Diagram

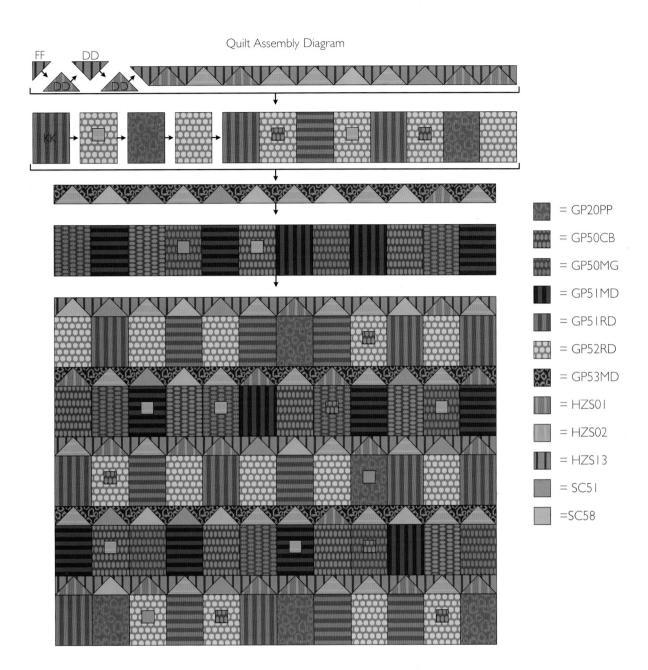

= GP20PP

= GP50CB

= GP50MG

= GP51MD

= GP51RD

= GP52RD

= GP53MD

= HZS01

= HZS02

= HZS13

= SC51

=SC58

give you 9 patches per 45in (114cm) wide fabric. Cut 12 in GP51RD, 6 in GP50MG, 4 in GP50CB and GP51MD.

Appliqué windows: Cut 1½in (3.75cm) squares. This includes a ¼ in (6mm) allowance. Cut 8 in GP50CB, HZS02 and 3 in SC51.

Binding: Cut 4 strips 2½in (6.5cm) wide × width of fabric in HZS07.

Backing: Cut 1 piece 46in x 44in (117cm x 112cm) in backing fabric.

MAKING THE BLOCKS
Use a ¼in (6mm) seam allowance throughout.

Press under a ¼in (6mm) allowance all round each window shape and appliqué by hand to the template KK rectangles as shown in the quilt assembly diagram. Referring to the quilt assembly diagram for fabric placement piece 7 'roof' rows and 7 'house' rows. Join the rows to form the quilt.

FINISHING THE QUILT
Press the quilt top. Layer the quilt top, batting and backing and baste together (see page 122). Using toning machine quilting thread, quilt in the ditch around all the house shapes. Trim the quilt edges and attach the binding (see page 122).

Cutting Diagram for Fabric HZS02

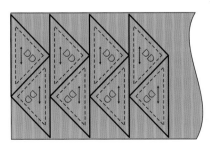

Told You So Baskets Quilt ★★

Mary Mashuta

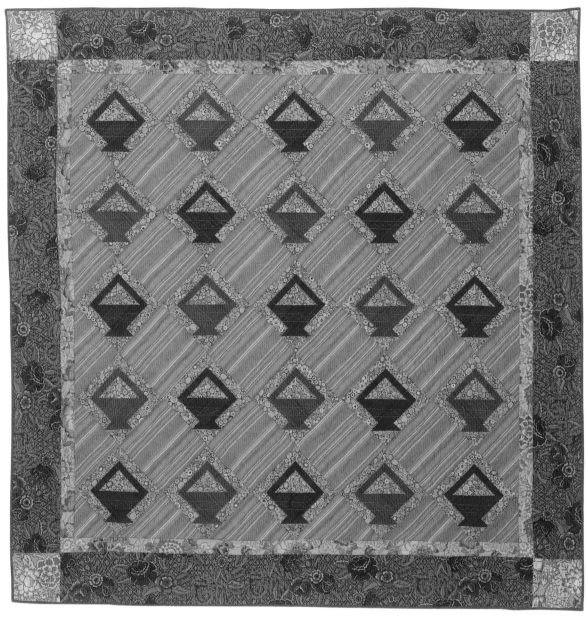

There are many ways stripes can be placed in this basket block. Mary tried them all. She ended up taking her sister Roberta's advice for once, because it would be easiest to 'speed cut' for quilters unaccustomed to 'fussy cutting' stripes.

SIZE OF QUILT
The finished quilt will measure approx.
81¾in x 81¾in (207.5cm x 207.5cm).

MATERIALS
Patchwork Fabrics:
PAPERWEIGHT
Algae   GP20AL: 1¾ yds (1.6m)
WOVEN HAZE STRIPE
Persimmon   HZS01: ½ yd (45cm)
Blush   HZS09: 2 yds (1.9m)

Scarlet   HZS18: ¾ yd (70cm)

Borders:
CLOISONNE
Aqua   GP46AQ: ⅝ yd (60cm)
Terracotta   GP46TC: ⅜ yd (35cm)
BURNT WOOD ROSE
Wine   GP47WN: 2 yds (1.9m)

Backing Fabric: 5¼ yds (4.8m)
We suggest these fabrics for backing:

CABBAGE & ROSES, Wine GP38WN
CLOISONNE, Terracotta GP46TC
BURNT WOOD ROSE, Wine GP47WN

Binding:
WOVEN HAZE STRIPE
Aegean   HZS20: ¾ yd (70cm)

Batting:
90in x 90in (229cm x 229cm).

Quilting thread:
Invisible and aqua machine quilting thread.

Templates:
see pages 111, 112

EE   CC   FF   GG   HH   II & Reverse II

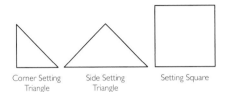
Corner Setting   Side Setting   Setting Square
Triangle   Triangle

PATCH SHAPES
The baskets blocks are made using 3 triangle patch shapes (Templates EE, CC &FF) and 3 lozenge patch shapes (Templates GG, HH and II & Reverse II). The blocks are set 'on point' alternated with 1 setting square patch shape, cut to size. The edges of the quilt centre are completed using 2 setting triangle patch shapes cut to size. The quilt is finished with an inner and outer border, both with corner posts.

CUTTING OUT
Important Information:
Please read carefully before cutting the stripe fabrics.
1. Stripe pattern placement is important graphically. (Don't worry about the grainline.) Consult the quilt assembly diagram and remember you can always turn your patch over as the stripe fabrics are reversible.
2. Open out the stripe fabric and cut one layer at a time.
3. Use a gridded ruler to get the first accurate cut across the fabric by lining up the stripe lines with ruler lines.
4. Keep checking that your cutting line is still perpendicular to the ruler edge as you cut.

Take time to correct, if necessary. This extra effort is worth it, and a little extra fabric has been allowed for you to 'true up' your stripes.

Template CC: Cut 3⅞in (9.75cm) wide strips across the width of the fabric. Each strip will give you 20 patches per 45in (114cm) wide fabric. Cut 75 in GP20AL.
Template EE: Cut 6⅞in (17.5cm) wide strips across the width of the fabric. Each strip will give you 12 patches per 45in (114cm) wide fabric. Cut 13 in HZS18 and 12 in HZS01.
Template FF: Cut 2⅜in (6cm) wide strips across the width of the fabric. Each strip will give you 34 patches per 45in (114cm) wide fabric. Cut 26 in HZS18 and 24 in HZS01.
Template GG: Cut 1⅜in (3.5cm) wide strips across the width of the fabric. Each strip will give you 6 patches per 45in (114cm) wide fabric. Cut 26 in HZS18 and 24 in HZS01.
Template HH: Cut 2 in (5cm) wide strips across the width of the fabric. Each strip will give you 4 patches per 45in (114cm) wide fabric. Cut 50 in GP20AL.

Block Assembly Diagrams

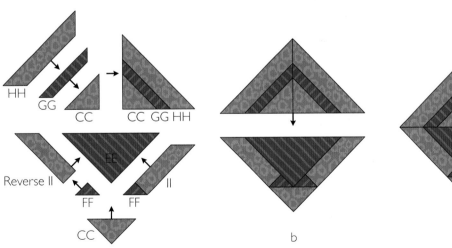

a   b   c

Template II & Reverse II: Cut 2 in (5cm) wide strips across the width of the fabric. Each strip will give you 7 patches per 45in (114cm) wide fabric. Cut 25 in GP20AL then flip the template over and cut a further 25 in GP20AL.

Setting Squares: Cut 9½in (24.25cm) wide strips across the width of the fabric. Each strip will give you 4 patches per 45in (114cm) wide fabric. From the strips cut 9½ in (24.25cm) squares. Cut 16 squares in HZS09.

Side Setting Triangles: Cut 9⅞ in (25cm) wide strips across the width of the fabric. Each strip will give you 8 patches per 45in (114cm) wide fabric. From the strips cut 8 x 9⅞ in (25cm) squares. Cut each square once diagonally to make 4 triangles. Cut 16 in HZS09.

Corner Setting Triangles: Cut 1 x 10¼in (26cm) square in HZS09. Cut the square twice diagonally to make 4 triangles.

Inner Border: Cut 7 strips 2½in (6.5cm) wide x width of fabric in GP46AQ. Join strips as necessary and cut 4 strips 64⅛in x 2½in (163cm x 6.5cm).

Outer Border: Cut 8 strips 7½in (19cm) wide x width of fabric in GP47WN. Join strips as necessary and cut 4 strips 68⅛in x 7½in (173cm x 19cm).

Corner Posts: Cut 4 x 2½in (6.5cm) squares and 4 x 7½in (19cm) squares in GP46TC. There is enough fabric to fussy cut these squares, choose mainly yellow areas for the small squares and varied colours for the larger squares.

Binding: Cut 9½ yds (8.7m) of 2½in (6.5cm) wide bias binding in HZS20.

Backing: Cut 2 pieces 45in x 90in (115cm x 229cm) in backing fabric.

MAKING THE BLOCKS

Use a ¼in (6mm) seam allowance throughout. Referring to the quilt assembly diagram for fabric placement piece 25 basket blocks following block assembly diagrams a and b, the finished block can be seen in diagram c.

MAKING THE QUILT

Lay the blocks out alternating with the setting squares and filling the edges and corners with the setting triangles. The stripe direction for all the setting pieces should run in the same direction, this will mean the quilt centre edges are on the bias and a bit stretchy, so handle it carefully. Separate into diagonal rows and join. Join the rows to complete the quilt centre as shown in the quilt assembly diagram. Join the side inner borders to the quilt centre, join a corner post to each end of the top and bottom inner borders and then join to the quilt centre. Join the outer borders to the quilt centre in the same way, as shown in the quilt assembly diagram.

FINISHING THE QUILT

Press the quilt top. Seam the backing pieces using a ¼in (6mm) seam allowance to form a piece approx. 90in x 90in (229cm x 229cm). Layer the quilt top, batting and backing and baste together (see page 122). Using invisible machine quilting thread, quilt in the ditch in the block and border seams. Quilt the baskets, setting squares, setting triangles, inner borders and corner posts using aqua machine quilting thread as shown in the quilting diagram. For the outer borders quilt in a diamond lattice following the pattern in the fabric print, again using the aqua thread. Trim the quilt edges and attach the binding (see page 122).

Quilting Diagram

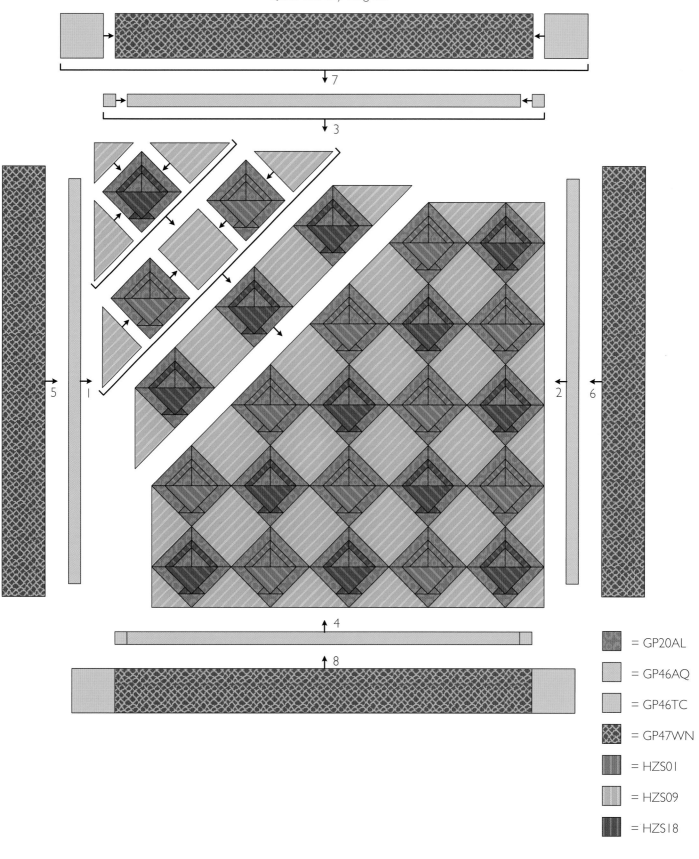

= GP20AL

= GP46AQ

= GP46TC

= GP47WN

= HZS01

= HZS09

= HZS18

Bottle Pinwheel Quilt ★

Kaffe Fassett

Of all the basic patchwork blocks this one has the most movement yet is so easy to sew. How different this dark and mysterious version is from its bright pastel counterpart Pastel Pinwheel.

SIZE OF QUILT
The finished quilt will measure approx. 51in x 44½in (129.5cm x 113cm).

MATERIALS
Patchwork Fabrics:

LAVA	
Red	CM01RD: ¼ yd (25cm)
Rust	CM01RU: ¼ yd (25cm)
MARBLE	
Turquoise	CM02TQ: ¼ yd (25cm)
FOSSIL	
Turquoise	CM03TQ: ¼ yd (25cm)

CHICKEN SCRATCH	
Black	CM05BK: ¼ yd (25cm)
Rust	CM05RU: ¼ yd (25cm)
Turquoise	CM05TQ: ¼ yd (25cm)
ROMAN GLASS	
Jungle	GP01JU: 1½yds (1.4m)
PAPERWEIGHT	
Algae	GP20AL: ¼ yd (25cm)
Gypsy	GP20GY: ¼ yd (25cm)
BEAD STRIPE	
Jungle	GP50JG: ¼ yd (25cm)
Moss	GP50MS: ¼ yd (25cm)

DOTTED LEAF	
Sage	LC03SA: ¼ yd (25cm)
SHOT COTTON	
Persimmon	SC07: ¼ yd (25cm)
Pomegranate	SC09: ¼ yd (25cm)
Aegean	SC46: ⅜ yd (35cm)
Grape	SC47: ¼ yd (25cm)

Backing Fabric: 3 yds (2.75m)
We suggest these fabrics for backing:
CHICKEN SCRATCH
Black CM05BK, Rust CM05RU or Turquoise CM05TQ

Binding:
AWNING STRIPE
Midnight   AWS06: ½ yd (45cm)

Batting:
59in x 52in (150 x 132cm).

Quilting thread:
Toning machine quilting thread.

Templates:
see page 108

PATCH SHAPES
Pinwheel blocks made using 1 triangle patch shape (Template F) are then alternated with a square patch shape (Template G) in a diagonal 'on point' setting. The quilt edges are completed with 2 triangle patch shapes, 1 for the quilt sides (Template H) and 1 for the quilt corners (Template I).

CUTTING OUT
Template F: Cut 3⅛in (8cm) wide strips across the width of the fabric. Each strip will give you 26 patches per 45in (114cm) wide fabric. Cut 3⅛in (8cm) squares, then cut diagonally to form 2 triangles using the template as a guide. Cut 48 in SC46, 32 in CM05BK, SC09, 28 in CM01RD, CM05TQ, GP20AL, GP20GY, SC07, 26 in CM03TQ, 24 in CM02TQ, GP50JG, GP50MS, SC47, 20 in CM01RU, CM05RU, LC03SA and 14 in GP01JU.
Template G: Cut 5in (12.75cm) wide strips across the width of the fabric. Each strip will

give you 8 patches per 45in (114cm) wide fabric. Cut 42 in GP01JU.

Template H: Cut 7⅝in (19.5cm) wide strips across the width of the fabric. Each strip will give you 20 patches per 45in (114cm) wide fabric. Cut 7 x 7⅝in (19.5cm) squares, then cut each square twice diagonally to make 4 triangles. This will ensure the long side of the triangle will not have a bias edge. Cut 26 in GP01JU.

Template I: Cut 4in (10.25cm) wide strips across the width of the fabric. Each strip will give you 10 patches per 45in (114cm) wide fabric. Cut 4in (10.25cm) squares, then cut diagonally to form 2 triangles using the template as a guide. Cut 4 in GP01JU.

Binding: Cut 5¾yds (5.25m) of 2½in (6.5cm) wide bias binding in AWS06.

Backing: Cut 1 piece 44in x 52in (112 x 132cm) and 1 piece 16in x 52in (40.5cm x 132cm) in backing fabric.

MAKING THE BLOCKS

Use a ¼in (6mm) seam allowance throughout. Piece 56 pinwheel blocks

following block assembly diagrams a and b. Refer to the quilt assembly diagram for fabric combinations. Note: there is 1 block on the left side of the quilt which uses 3 fabrics, all others use 2 per block.

MAKING THE QUILT

Lay out the blocks and alternate with the template G squares. Fill in the edges with the template H triangles and the corners with the template I triangles, as shown in the quilt assembly diagram. Separate into diagonal rows. Join the pieces to form the rows. Join the rows to complete the quilt top.

FINISHING THE QUILT

Press the quilt top. Seam the backing pieces using a ¼in (6mm) seam allowance to form a piece approx. 59in x 52in (150 x 132cm). Layer the quilt top, batting and backing and baste together (see page 122). Machine quilt as shown in the quilting diagram using toning thread. Trim the quilt edges and attach the binding (see page 122).

Block Assembly Diagrams

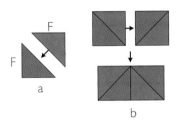

Quilting Diagram

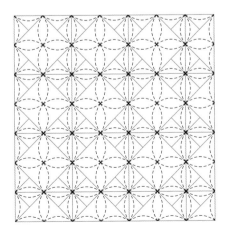

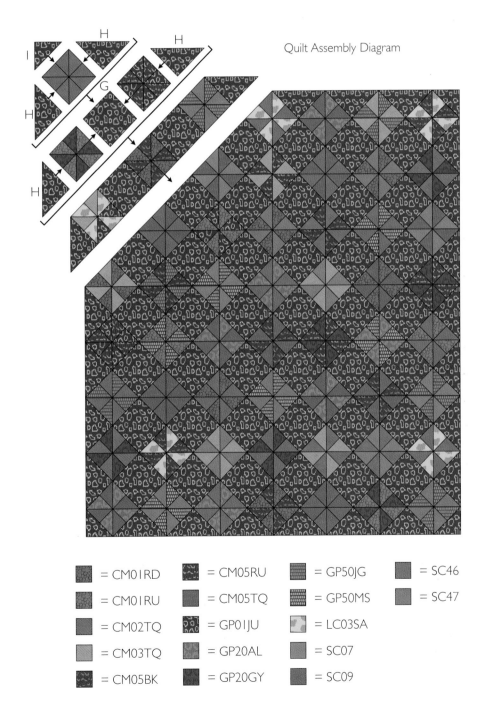

Quilt Assembly Diagram

= CM01RD	= CM05RU	= GP50JG	= SC46
= CM01RU	= CM05TQ	= GP50MS	= SC47
= CM02TQ	= GP01JU	= LC03SA	
= CM03TQ	= GP20AL	= SC07	
= CM05BK	= GP20GY	= SC09	

Pastel Pinwheel Quilt ★

KAFFE FASSETT

For this version of the Pinwheels quilt I chose bright pastels, quite a contrast to the more mysterious Bottle version. I like the way the many dotty fabrics play against each other.

SIZE OF QUILT
The finished quilt will measure approx. 51in × 44½in (129.5cm × 113cm).

MATERIALS
Patchwork Fabrics:

BATIK CONFETTI
Tomato	BKC01:	¼ yd (25cm)
Blue	BKC02:	¼ yd (25cm)
Slate	BKC04:	¼ yd (25cm)
Lilac	BKC06:	¼ yd (25cm)

LAVA
Blue	CM01BL:	¼ yd (25cm)

Pink	CM01PK:	¼ yd (25cm)
Red	CM01RD:	¼ yd (25cm)

CHICKEN SCRATCH
Rust	CM05RU:	¼ yd (25cm)
Shell	CM05SH:	¼ yd (25cm)

ROMAN GLASS
Dusky Pink	GP01DP:	¼ yd (25cm)
Red	GP01R:	¼ yd (25cm)

PAPERWEIGHT
Algae	GP20AL:	¼ yd (25cm)
Paprika	GP20PP:	¼ yd (25cm)
Pastel	GP20PT:	1½yds (1.4m)

PAISLEY STRIPE
Misty	GP32MS:	¼ yd (25cm)

SPOOLS
Lavender	GP34LV:	¼ yd (25cm)

DOTTED LEAF
French Blue	LC03FB:	¼ yd (25cm)

SHOT COTTON
Persimmon	SC07:	¼ yd (25cm)
Pomegranate	SC09:	¼ yd (25cm)
Chartreuse	SC12:	¼ yd (25cm)
Jade	SC41:	¼ yd (25cm)
Aegean	SC46:	¼ yd (25cm)

Backing Fabric: 3 yds (2.75m)
We suggest these fabrics for backing:
PAISLEY STRIPE, Misty GP32MS
SPOOLS, Lavender GP34LV
DOTTED LEAF, French Blue LC03FB

Binding:
LAVA
Red	CM01RD:	½ yd (45cm)

Batting:
59in × 52in (150 × 132cm).

Quilting thread:
Toning machine quilting thread.

Templates:
See Bottle Pinwheel Quilt.

PATCH SHAPES
See Bottle Pinwheel Quilt.

CUTTING OUT
Template F: Cut 3⅛in (8cm) wide strips across the width of the fabric. Each strip will give you 26 patches per 45in (114cm) wide fabric. Cut 3⅛in (8cm) squares, then cut diagonally to form 2 triangles using the template as a guide. Cut 46 in CM01BL. 36 in GP01DP, 28 in GP34LV, 26 in LC03FB, 24 in BKC06, GP32MS, SC07, SC09, SC41, 20 in CM01PK, GP20AL, SC12, SC46, 16 in BKC01, CM01RD, SC45, 12 in BKC02, CM05RU, CM05SH, GP20PP, 8 in BKC04 and GP01R.
Template G: Cut 5in (12.75cm) wide strips across the width of the fabric. Each strip will give you 8 patches per 45in (114cm) wide fabric. Cut 42 in GP20PT.
Template H: Cut 7⅝in (19.5cm) wide strips across the width of the fabric. Each strip will give you 20 patches per 45in (114cm) wide

fabric. Cut 7 × 7⅜in (19.5cm) squares, then cut each square twice diagonally to make 4 triangles. This will ensure the long side of the triangle will not have a bias edge. Cut 26 in GP20PT.

Template I: Cut 4in (10.25cm) wide strips across the width of the fabric. Each strip will give you 10 patches per 45in (114cm) wide fabric. Cut 4in (10.25cm) squares, then cut diagonally to form 2 triangles using the template as a guide. Cut 4 in GP20PT.

Binding: Cut 5 strips 2½in (6.5cm) wide × width of fabric in CM01RD.

Backing: Cut 1 piece 44in × 52in (112 × 132cm) and 1 piece 16in × 52in (40.5cm × 132cm) in backing fabric.

MAKING THE BLOCKS
See Bottle Pinwheel Quilt instructions. Note: there is 1 block on the bottom right corner of the quilt which uses 3 fabrics, all others use 2 per block.

MAKING THE QUILT
See Bottle Pinwheel Quilt instructions.

FINISHING THE QUILT
See Bottle Pinwheel Quilt instructions.

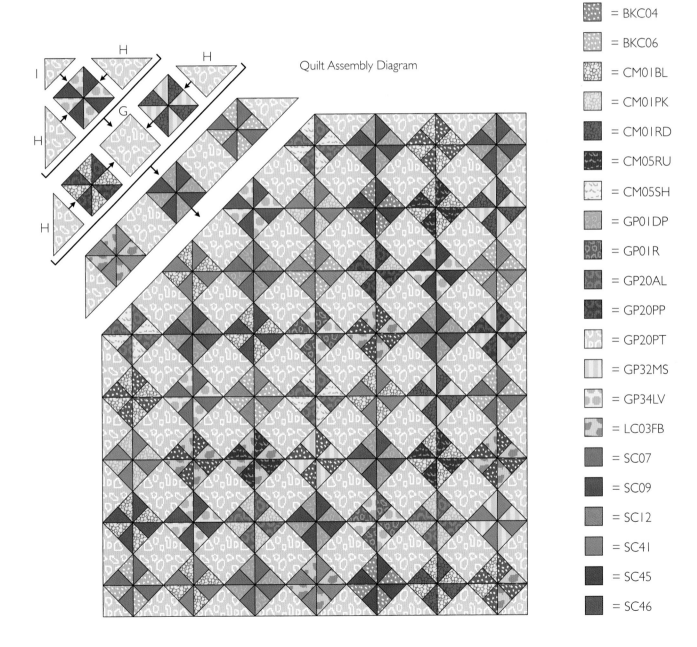

Quilt Assembly Diagram

▨	= BKC01
▨	= BKC02
▨	= BKC04
▨	= BKC06
▨	= CM01BL
▨	= CM01PK
▨	= CM01RD
▨	= CM05RU
▨	= CM05SH
▨	= GP01DP
▨	= GP01R
▨	= GP20AL
▨	= GP20PP
▨	= GP20PT
▨	= GP32MS
▨	= GP34LV
▨	= LC03FB
▨	= SC07
▨	= SC09
▨	= SC12
▨	= SC41
▨	= SC45
▨	= SC46

Spools Quilt ★★

PAULINE SMITH

Spools is one of my favourite blocks. In this version all the fabrics are prints, many from the new Philip Jacobs collection which I love.

SIZE OF QUILT
The finished quilt will measure approx. 78in × 60in (198cm × 152.5cm).

MATERIALS
Patchwork Fabrics:
BATIK CONFETTI
Lilac   BKC06: ⅜ yd (35cm)
CHICKEN SCRATCH
Mint   CM05MT: ¼ yd (25cm)

ROMAN GLASS
Dusty Pink   GP01DP: ¼ yd (25cm)
LOTUS LEAF
Blue   GP29BL: ½ yd (45cm)
FAN FLOWER
Lilac   GP36LI: ¼ yd (25cm)
EMBROIDERED LEAF
Taupe   GP42TA: ⅜ yd (35cm)
AURICULA
Gold   GP52GD: ¼ yd (25cm)

FLOWER SPRAYS
Gold   LC01GD: ⅜ yd (35cm)
                  or use leftover from borders.
DOTTED LEAF
Pink   LC03PK: ⅜ yd (35cm)
TRUMPET FLOWER
Green   PJ02GN: ¼ yd (25cm)
Grey   PJ02GY: ⅝ yd (60cm)
SHAGGY POPPY
Puce   PJ03PC: ⅝ yd (60cm)
Sage   PJ03SA: ⅜ yd (35cm)
CORAL
Pewter   PJ04PW: ¼ yd (25cm)
GERANIUM LEAF
Mint   PJ05MT: ⅜ yd (35cm)
Taupe   PJ05TA: ¼ yd (25cm)

Borders:
FLOWER SPRAYS
Gold   LC01GD: 2 yds (1.9m)

Backing Fabric: 3⅞ yds (3.6m)
We suggest these fabrics for backing:
FLOWER SPRAYS, Gold LC01GD
SHAGGY POPPY, Puce PJ03PC
TRUMPET FLOWER, Green PJ02GN

Binding:
GERANIUM LEAF
Mint   PJ05MT: ⅝ yd (60cm)

Batting:
86in × 68in (218.5cm × 173cm).

Quilting thread:
Deep coral quilting thread.

Templates:
see pages 107, 109, 113

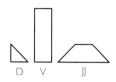

PATCH SHAPES
The spools blocks are made using 1 rectangle patch shape (Template V), 1 lozenge patch shape (Template JJ) and 1 triangle patch shape (Template D). The quilt is finished with a simple border.

CUTTING OUT
Borders: Along the length of the fabric cut 2 strips 6½in × 66½in × (16.5cm × 169cm) and

Block Assembly Diagrams

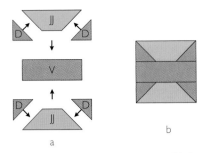

a   b

2 strips 6½in × 60½in × (16.5cm × 153.5cm)
in LC01GD. Reserve remaining fabric for
cutting template JJ.

Template D: Cut 2⅞in (7.25cm) wide strips
across the width of the fabric. Each strip will
give you 28 patches per 45in (114cm) wide
fabric. Cut 60 in PJ02GY, PJ03PC, 56 in
GP29BL, 48 in PJ03SA, 44 in BKC06, 36 in
GP42TA, 24 in PJ02GN and PJ04PW.
Template V: Cut 2½in (6.5cm) wide strips
across the width of the fabric. Each strip will
give you 6 patches per 45in (114cm) wide
fabric. Cut 15 in PJ02GY, PJ03PC, 14 in
GP29BL, 12 in PJ03SA, 11 in BKC06, 9 in
GP42TA, 6 in PJ02GN and PJ04PW.
Template JJ: Cut 2½in (6.5cm) wide strips
across the width of the fabric. Each strip will
give you 8 patches per 45in (114cm) wide
fabric. Cut 32 in LC01GD, 28 in LC03PK, 26
in PJ05MT, 24 in PJ05TA, 18 in CM05MT,
GP36LI, 16 in GP01DP and 14 in GP52GD.

Binding: Cut 7 strips 2½in (6.5cm) wide ×
width of fabric in PJ05MT.

Backing: Cut 2 pieces 43½in × 68in
(110.5cm × 173cm) in backing fabric.

MAKING THE BLOCKS
Use a ¼in (6mm) seam allowance
throughout. Referring to the quilt assembly
diagram for fabric placement piece 88 spools
blocks following block assembly diagram a,

Quilting Diagram

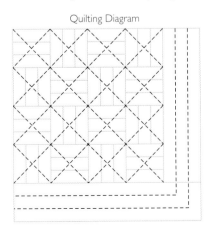

Quilt Assembly Diagram

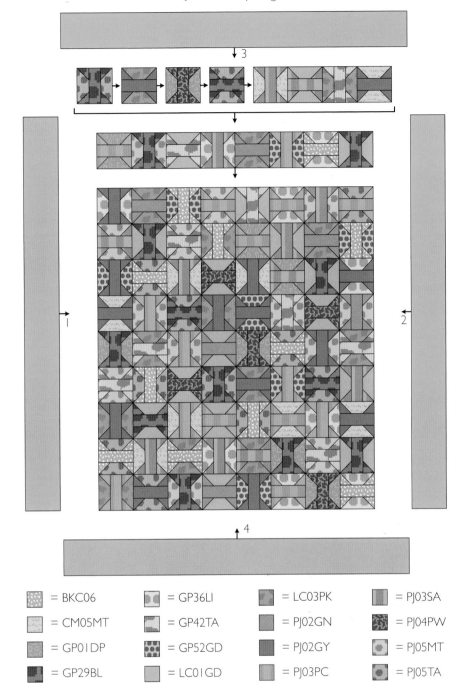

= BKC06   = GP36LI   = LC03PK   = PJ03SA

= CM05MT   = GP42TA   = PJ02GN   = PJ04PW

= GP01DP   = GP52GD   = PJ02GY   = PJ05MT

= GP29BL   = LC01GD   = PJ03PC   = PJ05TA

the finished block can be seen in diagram b.
MAKING THE QUILT
Join the blocks into 11 rows of 8 blocks. Join
the rows and add the border in the order
indicated in the quilt assembly diagram.

FINISHING THE QUILT
Press the quilt top. Seam the backing pieces
using a ¼in (6mm) seam allowance to

form a piece approx. 86in × 68in
(218.5cm × 173cm).
Layer the quilt top, batting and backing
and baste together (see page 122). Using
coral quilting thread, quilt as shown in the
quilting diagram by hand or machine. The
border quilting lines are spaced at 2in (5cm)
and 4in (10cm) from the border seam line.
Trim the quilt edges and attach the binding
(see page 122).

Pastel Ohio Star Quilt ★★

KAFFE FASSETT

Since I had done this layout of stars in strong contrast in Deep Ohio Star, I felt the urge to try it in a sweet pastel palette. The Harvest Toile print was a great starting point.

SIZE OF QUILT
The finished quilt will measure approx. 93¾in x 78¼in (238cm x 198.5cm).

MATERIALS
Patchwork Fabrics:
BATIK CONFETTI
Moss	BKC03:	¼ yd (25cm)
Lilac	BKC06:	½ yd (45cm)

CHICKEN SCRATCH
Fuchsia	CM05FU:	½ yd (45cm)
Mint	CM05MT:	¼ yd (25cm)

HARVEST TOILE
Fuchsia	GP35FU:	2¾ yds (2.5m)

FAN FLOWERS
California	GP36CA:	¼ yd (25cm)

DOTTED LEAF
French Blue	LC03FB:	⅜ yd (35cm)
Pink	LC03PK:	⅜ yd (35cm) or use leftover from border.

NOSEGAY
Gold	LC04GD:	⅜ yd (35cm)

MARIGOLD
Blue	MN07BL:	⅜ yd (35cm)
Pink	MN07PK:	⅜ yd (35cm)
Purple	MN07PU:	⅜ yd (35cm)

PLUMERIA
Pink	MN10PK:	½ yd (45cm)

SHOT COTTON
Tangerine	SC11:	½ yd (45cm)
Jade	SC41:	½ yd (45cm)

Borders:
DOTTED LEAF
Pink	LC03PK:	2½ yd (2.3m)

CORAL
Duck Egg	PJ04DE:	¾ yd (70cm)

Backing Fabric: 5¾ yds (5.3m)
We suggest these fabrics for backing:
DOTTED LEAF, Pink LC03PK
MARIGOLD, Purple MN07PU

Binding:
FAN FLOWER
Lilac	GP36LI:	¾ yd (70cm)

Batting:
102in x 86in (259cm x 218.5cm).

Quilting thread:
Toning machine quilting thread.

Templates:
see pages 110, 113, 117

PATCH SHAPES
The star blocks, which finish to 11in (28cm) are made using 2 square patch shapes (Templates SS & TT) and 2 triangle patch shapes (Templates UU, VV). The blocks are set 'on point' alternated with 1 setting square patch shape, cut to size. The edges of the quilt centre are completed using 2 setting triangle patch shapes cut to size (Side and Corner Setting Triangles). The quilt is finished with an inner and outer border.

CUTTING OUT

Template SS: Cut 6in (15.25cm) wide strips across the width of the fabric. Cut 4 in MN10PK, 3 in LC03FB, MN07PK, 2 in BKC06, LC03PK, LC04GD, MN07BL and MN07PU.

Template TT: Cut 3¼in (8.25cm) wide strips across the width of the fabric. Each strip will give you 12 patches per 45in (114cm) wide fabric. Cut 16 in CM05FU, SC11, SC41, 12 in CM05MT, 8 in BKC03, GP36CA and 4 in BKC06.

Template UU: Cut 3⅜in (8.5cm) wide strips across the width of the fabric. Each strip will give you 11 patches per 45in (114cm) wide fabric. Place the template with the long side along the cut edge of the strip, this will ensure the long side of the triangle will not have a bias edge. Cut 16 in CM05FU, SC11,

SC41, 12 in CM05MT, 8 in BKC03, GP36CA and 4 in BKC06.

Template VV: Cut 3⅝in (9.25cm) wide strips across the width of the fabric. Each strip will give you 22 patches per 45in (114cm) wide fabric. Cut 32 in MN10PK, 24 in LC03FB, MN07PK, 16 in BKC06, LC03PK, LC04GD, MN07BL and MN07PU.

Setting Squares: Cut 11½in (29.25cm) wide strips across the width of the fabric. Each strip will give you 3 patches per 45in (114cm) wide fabric. From the strips cut 11½ in (29.25cm) squares. Cut 12 in GP35FU.

Side Setting Triangles: Cut 17½in (44.5cm) wide strips across the width of the fabric. Each strip will give you 8 patches per 45in (114cm) wide fabric. Cut 4 x 17½in (44.5cm) squares, then cut each square twice diagonally

to make 4 triangles. This will ensure the long side of the triangle will not have a bias edge. These triangles are cut oversize and trimmed later. Cut 14 in GP35FU.

Corner Setting Triangles: Cut 2 x 9½in (24cm) squares in GP35FU. Cut each square once diagonally to make 2 triangles. These triangles are cut oversize and trimmed later.

Inner Border: Cut 8 strips 3in (7.75cm) wide x width of fabric in PJ04DE. Join strips as necessary and cut 2 strips 78¼in x 3in (198.75cm x 7.75cm) and 2 strips 67¾in x 3in (172cm x 7.75cm).

Outer Border: Cut from the length of the fabric 2 strips 83¼in x 6in (211.5cm x 15.25cm) and 2 strips 78¾in x 6in (200cm x 15.25cm) in LC03PK.

Binding: cut 9 strips 2½in (6.5cm) wide x width of fabric in GP36LI.

Backing: Cut 2 pieces 43½in x 102in (110.5cm x 259cm) in backing fabric.

Block Assembly Diagrams

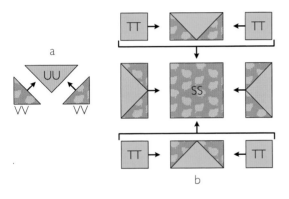

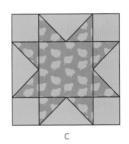

b

c

Quilting Diagram

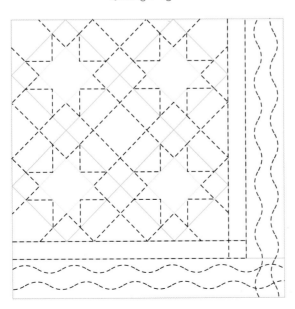

MAKING THE BLOCKS

Use a ¼in (6mm) seam allowance throughout. Referring to the quilt assembly diagram for fabric placement piece 20 star blocks following block assembly diagrams a and b, the finished block can be seen in diagram c.

MAKING THE QUILT

Lay the blocks out alternating with the setting squares and filling the edges and corners with the setting triangles. Separate into diagonal rows and join. Join the rows to complete the quilt centre as shown in the quilt assembly diagram. As the corner and side setting triangles were cut oversize, trim the quilt centre to ¼in (6mm) OUTSIDE the star block points. Join the side, then top and bottom inner borders to the quilt centre. Join the outer borders to the quilt centre in the same way, as indicated in the quilt assembly diagram.

FINISHING THE QUILT

Press the quilt top. Seam the backing pieces using a ¼in (6mm) seam allowance to form a piece approx. 102in x 86in (259cm x 218.5cm). Layer the quilt top, batting and backing and baste together (see page 122). Using toning machine quilting thread, quilt the centre section as shown in the quilting diagram. The borders are meander quilted, free motion style, following the leaf pattern in the fabric print. Trim the quilt edges and attach the binding (see page 122).

Quilt Assembly Diagram

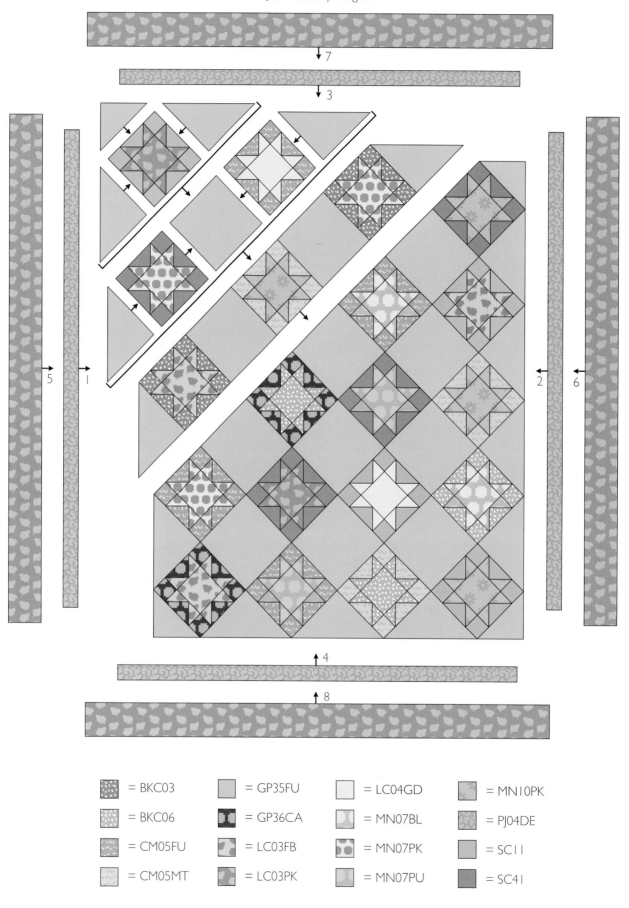

	= BKC03		= GP35FU		= LC04GD		= MN10PK
	= BKC06		= GP36CA		= MN07BL		= PJ04DE
	= CM05FU		= LC03FB		= MN07PK		= SC11
	= CM05MT		= LC03PK		= MN07PU		= SC41

Deep Ohio Star Quilt ★★

KAFFE FASSETT

I came across an opera of a quilt from the late 1800's called Evening Star. It had rich Victorian chintzes, deep jewel colours and high pastels for the contrast. Our large floral & fruit prints work a treat to recreate the mood.

SIZE OF QUILT
The finished quilt will measure approx.
103¾in x 83¾in (263.5cm x 212.75cm).

MATERIALS
Patchwork Fabrics:
BATIK CONFETTI
Slate	BKC04: ¼ yd (25cm)
Lilac	BKC06: ½ yd (45cm)

DOT CUBE
Blue	CM04BL: ¼ yd (25cm)
Fuchsia	CM04FU: ¼ yd (25cm)
Rust	CM04RU: ¼ yd (25cm)

CHICKEN SCRATCH
Pink	CM05PK: ¼ yd (25cm)

FOLIAGE
Black	DW02BK: ⅜ yd (35cm)

Jewel	DW02JW: ⅜ yd (35cm)

RENAISSANCE LEAF
Purple	DW05PU: ½ yd (45cm)

EMBROIDERED LEAF
Black	GP42BK: ⅝ yd (60cm)
Plum	GP42PL: ⅝ yd (60cm)

CLOISONNE
Black	GP46BK: ⅝ yd (60cm)

Teal   GP46TE: 1 yd (90cm)
FLOWER BASKET
Black   GP48BK: ½ yd (45cm)
Cobalt   GP48CB: ½ yd (45cm)
Magenta   GP48MG: ¼ yd (25cm)
DOTTED LEAF
Gold   LC03GD: ¼ yd (25cm)
Sage   LC03SA: ¼ yd (25cm)

Borders:
FLOWER BASKET
Rust   GP48RU: 3 yds (2.75m)
BEAD STRIPE
Jungle   GP50JG: 1 yd (90cm)

Backing Fabric: 6⅜ yds (5.8m)
We suggest these fabrics for backing:
EMBROIDERED LEAF, Plum GP42PL
FLOWER BASKET, Black GP48BK
FOLIAGE, Jewel DW02JW

Binding:
AWNING STRIPE
Lilac   AWS04: 1 yd (90cm)

Batting:
112in × 90in (284.5cm × 228.5cm).

Quilting thread:
Toning machine quilting thread.

Templates:
See Pastel Ohio Star Quilt

PATCH SHAPES
The star blocks, which finish to 11in (28cm) are made using 2 square patch shapes (Templates SS & TT) and 2 triangle patch shapes (Templates UU, VV). The blocks are set 'on point' alternated with 1 setting square patch shape, cut to size. The edges of the quilt centre are completed using 2 setting triangle patch shapes cut to size (Side and Corner Setting Triangles). The side inner borders are simply cut to size from the length of the fabric, the top and bottom inner borders are pieced from 'fussy cut' rectangles cut to size, each rectangle is cut to centre on a basket in the fabric print. The quilt is finished with an outer border.

CUTTING OUT
Note: Some of the patch shapes for this quilt are large, therefore, to reduce waste, we suggest drawing round the templates for each patch shape onto the fabrics for the best fit before cutting.

Setting Squares: Cut 11½in (29.25cm) squares. Cut 2 in DW05PU, GP46BK, GP48CB, 1 in DW02BK, DW02JW, GP42BK, GP42PL, GP46TE and GP48BK.

Side Setting Triangles: To make a paper template cut a 12½in (31.75cm) square. Fold the square diagonally to form a right-angle triangle. The straight grain of the fabric must run along the long side of the triangle, this will ensure the long side of the triangle will not have a bias edge. These triangles are cut oversize and trimmed later. Cut 5 in GP46TE, 3 in GP42BK, GP46BK, 2 in GP42PL and 1 in GP48BK.

Corner Setting Triangles: Cut 1 × 9½in (24cm) square in GP42BK, GP42PL and GP46BK, cut each square diagonally to form 2 triangles. These triangles are cut oversize and trimmed later. Used in quilt: 2 in GP42PL, 1 in GP42BK and GP46BK.

Template SS: Cut 6in (15.25cm) wide strips across the width of the fabric. Cut 4 in GP46TE, 2 in DW02BK, DW02JW, DW05PU, GP42PL, GP48BK, GP48CB, GP48MG, 1 in GP42BK and GP46BK.

Template TT: Cut 3¼in (8.25cm) wide strips across the width of the fabric. Each strip will give you 12 patches per 45in (114cm) wide fabric. Cut 16 in BKC06, 12 in CM04BL, CM04FU, LC03GD, LC03SA, 8 in BKC04, 4 in CM04RU and CM05PK.

Template UU: Cut 3⅜in (8.5cm) wide strips across the width of the fabric. Each strip will give you 11 patches per 45in (114cm) wide fabric. Place the template with the long side along the cut edge of the strip, this will ensure the long side of the triangle will not have a bias edge. Cut 16 in BKC06, 12 in CM04BL, CM04FU, LC03GD, LC03SA, 8 in BKC04, 4 in CM04RU and CM05PK.

Template VV: Cut 3⅝in (9.25cm) wide strips across the width of the fabric. Each strip will give you 22 patches per 45in (114cm) wide fabric. Cut 32 in GP46TE, 16 in DW02BK, DW02JW, DW05PU, GP42PL, GP48BK, GP48CB, GP48MG, 8 in GP42BK and GP46BK.

Inner Border: In GP48RU cut 2 strips 9¼in × 78¼in (23.5cm × 198.75cm) from the length of the fabric, these strips must be cut along each of the selvedge edges of the fabric. From the remaining centre section of fabric 'fussy cut' rectangles, centring each on one basket design. In all cases the 11½in

(29.25cm) measurement is the vertical size. Cut 2 rectangles 11½in × 12in (29.25cm × 30.5cm) and 12 rectangles 11½in × 11⅞in (29.25cm × 30.25cm).

Outer Border: Cut 2½in (6.5cm) strips from the length of the fabric. Join the strips, matching the stripe pattern, to form 2 strips 2½in × 100¼in (6.5cm × 254.75cm) and 2 strips 2½in × 84¼in (6.5cm × 214cm) in GP50JG.

Binding: Cut 10¾yds (9.8m) of 2½in (6.5cm) wide bias binding in AWS04.

Backing: Cut 2 pieces 45in × 112in (114.5cm × 284.5cm) in backing fabric.

MAKING THE BLOCKS
See Pastel Ohio Star Quilt instructions.

MAKING THE QUILT CENTRE
Lay the blocks out alternating with the setting squares and filling the edges and corners with the setting triangles. Separate into diagonal rows and join. Join the rows to complete the quilt centre as shown in the quilt assembly diagram. As the corner and side setting triangles were cut oversize, trim the quilt centre to ¼in (6mm) OUTSIDE the star block points.

MAKING THE BORDERS
Join the side borders to the trimmed quilt centre. To make the top and bottom inner borders lay out the 'fussy cut' rectangles with the baskets all vertical. Join into 2 rows of 7 rectangles, with a slightly larger 11½in × 12in (29.25cm × 30.5cm) rectangle at the centre of each row. Join the pieced borders to the quilt centre. Join the outer border as indicated in the quilt assembly diagram.

FINISHING THE QUILT
Press the quilt top. Seam the backing pieces using a ¼in (6mm) seam allowance to form a piece approx. 112in × 90in (284.5cm × 228.5cm). Layer the quilt top, batting and backing and baste together (see page 122). Using toning machine quilting thread, quilt the centre section as shown in the quilting diagram for Pastel Ohio Star Quilt on page 87. The borders are meander quilted, free motion style, following the basket pattern in the fabric print. Trim the quilt edges and attach the binding (see page 122).

Quilt Assembly Diagram

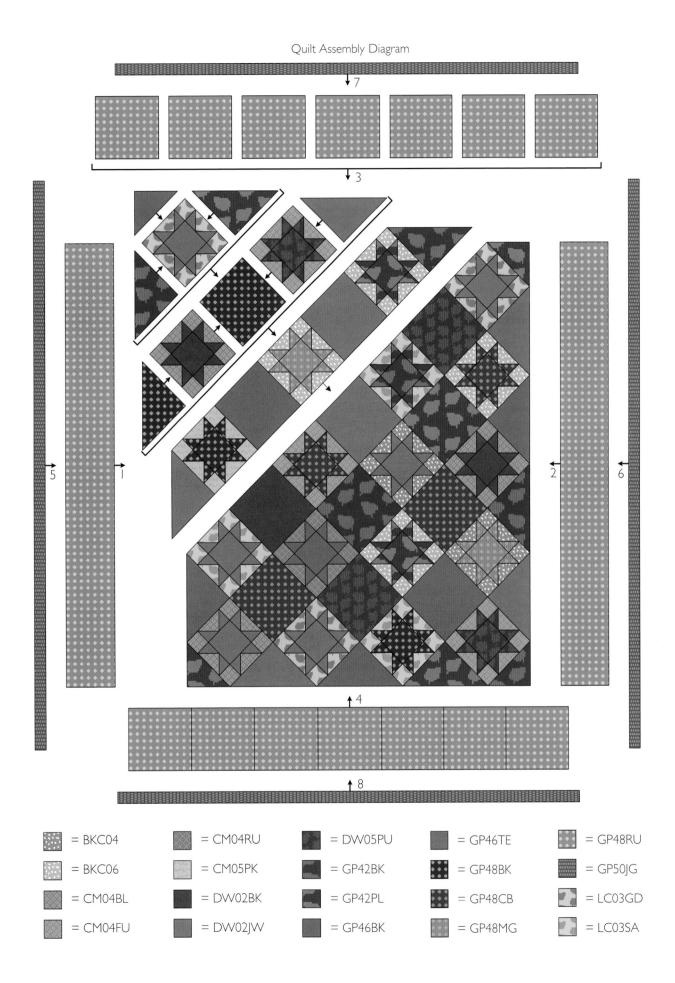

= BKC04   = CM04RU   = DW05PU   = GP46TE   = GP48RU

= BKC06   = CM05PK   = GP42BK   = GP48BK   = GP50JG

= CM04BL   = DW02BK   = GP42PL   = GP48CB   = LC03GD

= CM04FU   = DW02JW   = GP46BK   = GP48MG   = LC03SA

New Orleans Star Quilt ★★

LIZA PRIOR-LUCY

About the time I was ready to begin a new quilt for this book I found this complex and interesting star block. Unfolding on my television as I was working out the pattern were the images of the destruction of New Orleans and the unbelievable horror of seeing people trying to withstand the storm and its aftermath. I hadn't really considered how those images had entered my consciousness until I was well into sewing this quilt. Here are the colours of storms, oil slicks, dark waters and mystery. There are also glimpses of light and hopeful things.

SIZE OF QUILT

The finished quilt will measure approx. 69in x 57in (175cm x 145cm).

MATERIALS

Patchwork Fabrics:

LAYERED TWIRLS
Lavender	CM06LV: ⅛ yd (15cm)
Mauve	CM06MV: ¼ yd (25cm)
Sea Green	CM06SG: ¼ yd (25cm)

ROOTLETS
Black	CM07BK: ¼ yd (25cm)
Brown	CM07BR: ¼ yd (25cm)
Lavender	CM07LV: ⅛ yd (15cm)
Mauve	CM07MV: ⅜ yd (35cm)
Sea Green	CM07SG: ¼ yd (25cm)

STARSHINE
Black	CM08BK: ¼ yd (25cm)
Mauve	CM08MV: ⅜ yd (35cm)
Sea Green	CM08SG: ¼ yd (25cm)

FEATHER
Mauve	CM09MV: ¼ yd (25cm)
Sea Green	CM09SG: ⅜ yd (35cm)

SWIRL MINI
Black	CM10BK: ¼ yd (25cm)
Blue	CM10BL: ¼ yd (25cm)
Lavender	CM10LV: ¼ yd (25cm)
Mauve	CM10MV: ¼ yd (25cm)
Rose	CM10RO: ¼ yd (25cm)
Sea Green	CM10SG: ¼ yd (25cm)

BAS-RELIEF
Moss	DW01MS: ¼ yd (25cm)

FOLIAGE
Black	DW02BK: ¼ yd (25cm)

TAPESTRY
Brown	DW03BR: ⅜ yd (35cm)

MEDIEVAL ROSE
Leafy	DW04LF: ¼ yd (25cm)

RENAISSANCE LEAF
Brown	DW05BR: ¼ yd (25cm)
Moss	DW05MS: ¼ yd (25cm)
Purple	DW05PU: ¼ yd (25cm)

NOSEGAY
Taupe	LC04TA: ¼ yd (25cm)

ARBOUR
Taupe	LC05TA: ¼ yd (25cm)

ROMAN GLASS
Jungle	GP01JU: ¼ yd (25cm)

PUFF
Peat	GP43PA: ¼ yd (25cm)

ISLANDS
Moss	GP49MS: ¼ yd (25cm)

SHIRT STRIPES
Soft	GP51SF: ¼ yd (25cm)

AURICULA
Olive	GP52OV: ¼ yd (25cm)

DAHLIA BLOOMS
Autumn	GP54AT: ¼ yd (25cm)
Succulent	GP54SC: ¼ yd (25cm)

PLUMS
Summer Delight	MN12SD: ¼ yd (25cm)

PANSY
Oxblood	PJ01OX: ¼ yd (25cm)

TRUMPET FLOWER
Black	PJ02BK: ¼ yd (25cm)

Borders:

GERANIUM LEAF
Sludge	PJ05SL: 1 yd (90cm)

Backing Fabric: 3¾ yds (3.4m)
We suggest these fabrics for backing:
PUFF, Peat GP43PA
TRUMPET FLOWER, Black PJ02BK
FOLIAGE, Black DW02BK.

Binding:
SINGLE IKAT FEATHERS
Turquoise	SIF04: ¾ yd (70cm)

Batting:
77in x 65in (195.5cm x 165cm).

Quilting thread:
Mauve machine quilting thread.

Templates:
see pages 111, 116, 118

PATCH SHAPES

Three square patch shapes (Template Z, AA & BB) and two triangle patch shapes (Template CC & DD) are pieced to make star blocks for the quilt centre. The quilt is finished with a simple border.

CUTTING OUT

For the best use of the fabric cut the large template shapes first, then trim remaining fabric strips for smaller shapes. We have listed the template shapes in order of size to help with this.

Template Z: Cut 4¾in (12cm) wide strips across the width of the fabric. Each strip will give you 8 patches per 45in (114cm) wide fabric. Cut 4 in GP54AT, 3 in GP52OV, GP54SC, 2 in DW02BK, DW05MS, DW05PU, PJ02BK, 1 in DW05BR and MN12SD.

Template DD: Cut 4¼in (10.75cm) wide

Block Assembly Diagrams

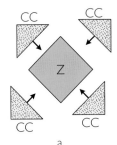

a

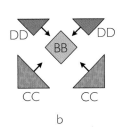

b

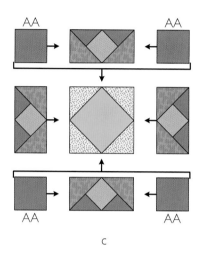

c

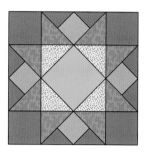

d

strips across the width of the fabric. Each strip will give you 36 patches per 45in (114cm) wide fabric. Cut 4¼in (10.75cm) squares, then using the template as a guide cut each square twice diagonally to make 4 triangles. This will ensure the long side of the triangle will not have a bias edge. Cut 16 in DW03BR, 8 in CM06MV, CM06SG, CM07BK, CM07BR, CM07MV, CM07SG, CM08MV, CM08SG, CM09MV, CM09SG, CM10BL, DW01MS, DW04LF, DW05MS, GP01JU, GP51SF, PJ01OX and PJ02BK.

Template CC: Cut 3⅞in (9.75cm) wide strips across the width of the fabric. Each strip will give you 20 patches per 45in (114cm) wide fabric. Cut 16 in CM10MV, 12 in CM07LV, CM07MV, CM08BK, CM08MV, CM09SG, CM10RO, CM10SG, DW01MS, LC05TA, GP49MS, 8 in CM06LV, CM07BK, CM07BR, CM09MV, CM10BL, CM10LV, DW03BR, LC04TA, GP01JU, GP43PA, GP51SF, 4 in CM06MV, CM10BK, DW04LF and PJ01OX.

Template AA: Cut 3½in (9cm) wide strips across the width of the fabric. Each strip will give you 12 patches per 45in (114cm) wide

fabric. Cut 8 in DW03BR, 4 in CM06MV, CM06SG, CM07BK, CM07BR, CM07MV, CM07SG, CM08MV, CM08SG, CM09MV, CM09SG, CM10BL, DW01MS, DW04LF, DW05MS, GP01JU, GP51SF, PJ01OX and PJ02BK.

Template BB: Cut 2⅝in (6.75cm) wide strips across the width of the fabric. Each strip will give you 16 patches per 45in (114cm) wide fabric. Cut 12 in DW01MS, 8 in CM08BK, CM10RO, GP43PA, GP49MS, MN12SD, 4 in CM07MV, CM10BK, CM10LV, CM10SG, LC04TA, LC05TA and PJ01OX.

Border: Cut 6 strips 5in (12.75cm) wide × width of fabric in PJ05SL. Join strips as necessary and cut 2 strips 60½in × 5in (153.75cm × 12.75cm) for the side borders and 2 strips 57½in × 5in (146cm × 12.75cm) for the top and bottom borders.

Binding: Cut 7¼yds (7.5m) of 2½in (6.5cm) wide bias binding in SIF04.

Backing: Cut 1 piece 42in × 65in (107cm × 165cm) and 1 piece 36in × 65in (91.5cm ×

165cm) in backing fabric.

MAKING THE BLOCKS
Use a ¼in (6mm) seam allowance throughout. Piece 20 blocks following block assembly diagrams a, b and c, the completed block is shown in diagram d. Refer to the quilt assembly diagram for fabric placement.

MAKING THE QUILT
Piece the blocks together into 5 rows of 4 blocks, join the rows to make the quilt centre. Join the side, then top and bottom borders to the quilt centre as shown in the quilt assembly diagram.

FINISHING THE QUILT
Press the quilt top. Seam the backing pieces using a ¼in (6mm) seam allowance to form a piece approx. 77in × 65in (195.5cm × 165cm). Layer the quilt top, batting and backing and baste together (see page 122). Using mauve machine quilting thread, quilt in a 'twirly' pattern over the quilt centre and borders. Trim the quilt edges and attach the binding (see page 122).

Quilt Assembly Diagram

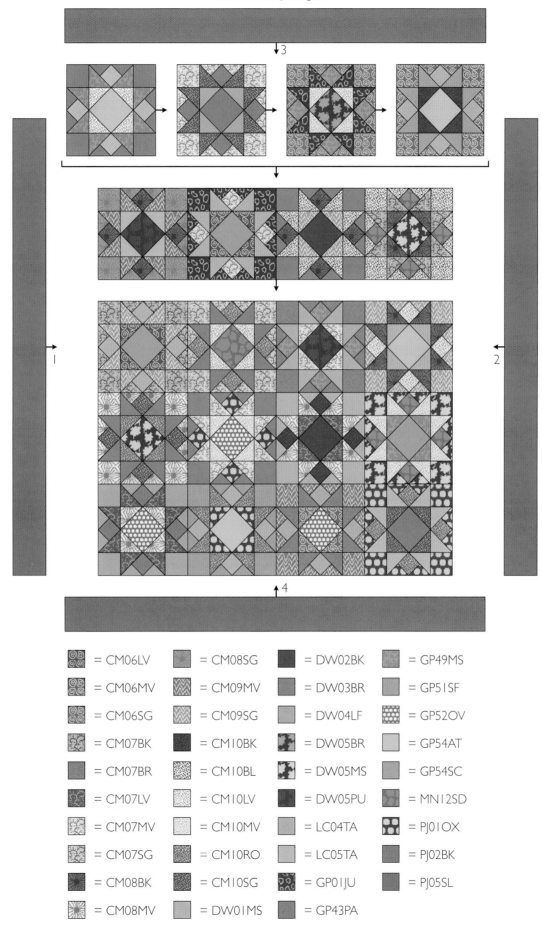

= CM06LV	= CM08SG	= DW02BK	= GP49MS
= CM06MV	= CM09MV	= DW03BR	= GP51SF
= CM06SG	= CM09SG	= DW04LF	= GP52OV
= CM07BK	= CM10BK	= DW05BR	= GP54AT
= CM07BR	= CM10BL	= DW05MS	= GP54SC
= CM07LV	= CM10LV	= DW05PU	= MN12SD
= CM07MV	= CM10MV	= LC04TA	= PJ01OX
= CM07SG	= CM10RO	= LC05TA	= PJ02BK
= CM08BK	= CM10SG	= GP01JU	= PJ05SL
= CM08MV	= DW01MS	= GP43PA	

Broken Dishes Quilt ★ ★ ★

Kaffe Fassett

Years ago I was honoured by an invitation to view the quilts archived at the Royal Ontario Museum in Toronto. My most vivid memory was opening a drawer to glimpse a fantastic version of Broken Dishes. In a book called 'The American Quilt' (Potter) I discovered a 1950 Broken Dishes done in large blocks of similar combinations. I loved constructing my lay out and find a deep satisfaction in working with smaller pieces than usual. Pauline Smith, who sewed it together, may have had other feelings on the matter!

SIZE OF QUILT
The finished quilt will measure approx.
81in × 72in (206cm × 183cm).

MATERIALS
Patchwork Fabrics:
BATIK CONFETTI
Tomato   BKC01: ⅜ yd (35cm)

Blue   BKC02: ¾ yd (70cm)
Moss   BKC03: ⅜ yd (35cm)
Slate   BKC04: ⅝ yd (60cm)
FOSSIL
Blue   CM03BL: ⅝ yd (60cm)
Rust   CM03RU: ¾ yd (70cm)
DOT CUBE
Blue   CM04BL: ⅞ yd (80cm)

CHICKEN SCRATCH
Fuchsia   CM05FU: ⅝ yd (60cm)
Mint   CM05MT: ⅞ yd (80cm)
Pink   CM05PK: ½ yd (45cm)
Rust   CM05RU: ⅜ yd (35cm)
Shell   CM05SH: ⅞ yd (80cm)
Turquoise   CM05TQ: ⅝ yd (60cm)
ROMAN GLASS
Dusty Pink   GP01DP: ⅝ yd (60cm)
PAPERWEIGHT
Gypsy   GP20GY: ⅜ yd (35cm)
Teal   GP20TE: ½ yd (45cm)
FRECKLES
Gold   GP40GD: ⅝ yd (60cm)
Pink   GP40PK: ⅞ yd (80cm)
FLOWER SPRAYS
Gold   LC01GD: ⅝ yd (60cm)
Periwinkle   LC01PE: ⅝ yd (60cm)

Backing Fabric
Note: The backing for this quilt was pieced from the 5 fabrics listed below, alternatively use 4⅝ yds (4.25m) of any one of the fabrics.
CHICKEN SCRATCH
Fuchsia   CM05FU: 1⅛ yd (1m)
Mint   CM05MT: 1⅛ yd (1m)
ROMAN GLASS
Dusty Pink   GP01DP: 1⅛ yd (1m)
FRECKLES
Pink   GP40PK: 1⅛ yd (1m)
FLOWER SPRAYS
Gold   LC01GD: 1⅛ yd (1m)

Binding:
Pieced from remnants.

Batting:
88in × 80in (223.5cm × 203cm).

Quilting thread:
Toning hand quilting thread.

PATCH SHAPES
No templates are given for this quilt as 2 sizes of '4 triangle units' are pieced using squares cut to size. Full instructions on how to piece the '4 triangle units' are given opposite. The small '4 triangle units', which finish to 2¼in (5.7cm), are pieced into blocks for the quilt centre. The large '4 triangle units', which finish to 4½in (11.4cm), are pieced to form the quilt border.

CUTTING OUT

Note: Cut the large squares first, then trim and use any remaining strips for the small squares.

Large Squares for Border Blocks: Cut 5¾in (14.6cm) wide strips across the width of the fabric. Cut the strips into 5¾in (14.6cm) squares, each strip will give you 7 squares per 45in (114cm) wide fabric. Cut 10 squares in BKC02, 9 in CM05SH, GP40PK, 8 in CM03RU, CM04BL, CM05MT, 7 in BKC04, CM03BL, CM05FU, GP40GD, LC01GD, LC01PE, 6 in CM05PK, GP01DP, GP20TE, 5 in BKC03 and 3 in CM05TQ. Total: 120 squares.

Small Squares for Centre Blocks: Cut 3½in (8.9cm) wide strips across the width of the fabric. Cut the strips into 3½in (8.9cm) squares, each strip will give you 12 squares per 45in (114cm) wide fabric. Cut 53 squares in CM05MT, 52 in CM04BL, CM05SH, 47 in GP40PK, 45 in CM05TQ, 41 in BKC02, 39 in GP01DP, 36 in BKC01, CM05FU, 34 in GP40GD, 29 in LC01PE, 28 in CM03BL, CM03RU, 27 in GP20GY, 26 in CM05RU, 25 in BKC04, LC01GD, 22 in GP20TE, 18 in CM05PK and 15 in BKC03. Total: 678 squares.

Binding: Cut 2½in (6.5cm) wide strips from remnants, join to make 8¾ yds (8m) of 2½in (6.5cm) wide binding.

Backing: For single fabric backing cut 2 pieces 44in × 80in (112cm × 203cm) in backing fabric. For pieced backing cut 1 piece 18in × 44in (46cm × 112cm) and 1 piece 18in × 39in (46cm × 99cm) in CM05FU, CM05MT, GP01DP, GP40PK and LC01GD.

MAKING THE '4 TRIANGLE UNITS'

Use a ¼in (6mm) seam allowance throughout, it is essential that the seam allowance is accurate and consistent for these units. Refer to the centre blocks diagram for fabric combinations for the centre blocks and the quilt assembly diagram for the border blocks. Most of the blocks have 2 or 3 'main' fabrics and 1 or more 'highlight' fabrics.

The method given will make 2 identical '4 triangle units' from each pair of squares. Each unit will have 2 triangles of each fabric. If you want to make a unit with 3 or 4 different fabrics make the units to stage 3, then combine parts from 2 different pairs of squares. Note: Some fabrics are used wrong side facing, to give a softer look, these are marked in the diagrams with a white circle.

Take 2 squares of different fabric, place right sides together matching the edges accurately. Mark a diagonal line from corner to corner with a soft pencil or washable marker, this will be the cutting line. Stitch the squares ¼in (6mm) from both sides of the cutting line as shown in sewing diagram a.

Cut along the marked cutting line to separate the 2 pieced squares, press the seam allowance towards the darker fabric as shown in sewing diagram b.

Take the 2 pieced squares and place them right sides together matching the seam lines accurately. Mark a diagonal line from corner to corner at right angles to the previous sewing line as shown in sewing diagram c, this will be the cutting line. Stitch the squares ¼ in (6mm) from both sides of the cutting line as before. Cut along the marked cutting line to separate the 2 '4 triangle units', press the seam allowance to one side as shown in sewing diagram d.

Sewing Diagrams

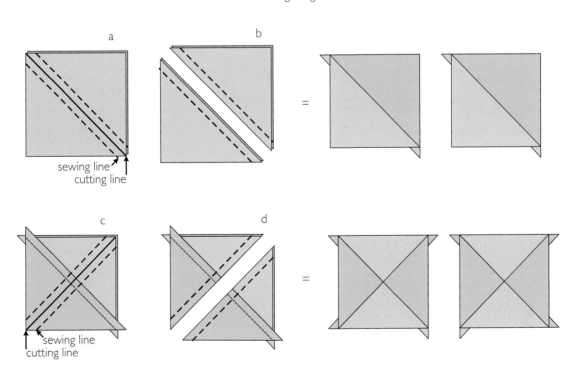

a

sewing line
cutting line

b

=

c

sewing line
cutting line

d

=

MAKING THE BLOCKS

For each centre block (finish to 9in (22.9cm)) take 16 small '4 triangle units'. Piece into rows, then join the rows to form the blocks as shown in the centre block assembly diagram. Make 42 blocks as shown in the centre blocks diagram. For each border block (finish to 9in (22.9cm)) take 4 large '4 triangle units' and piece as shown in the border block assembly diagram. Make 30 blocks as shown in the quilt assembly diagram.

MAKING THE QUILT

Piece the centre blocks into 7 rows of 6 blocks as shown in the quilt assembly diagram. Join the rows to form the quilt centre. Piece the border blocks into two 7 block rows for the sides of the quilt and two 8 block rows for the top and bottom of the quilt. Join the borders to the quilt centre as indicated in the quilt assembly diagram.

FINISHING THE QUILT

Press the quilt top. For single fabric backing seam the 2 backing pieces using a ¼in (6mm) seam allowance to form a piece approx. 88in × 80in (223.5cm × 203cm). For pieced backing join the 2 pieces of each fabric to form a long strip. In the order indicated in the backing diagram join the strips, staggering the seams as shown. Layer the quilt top, batting and backing and baste together (see page 122). Using toning hand quilting thread quilt in the ditch along the diagonal seam lines as shown in the quilting diagram. Trim the quilt edges and attach the binding (see page 122).

Centre Block Assembly Diagram

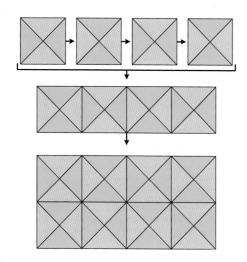

Border Block Assembly Diagram

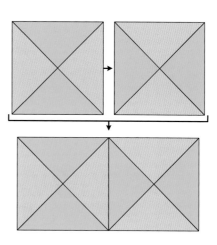

Quilting Diagram

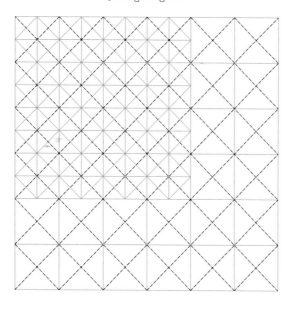

Backing Diagram

CM05MT	
LC01GD	
GP40PK	
GP01DP	
CM05FU	

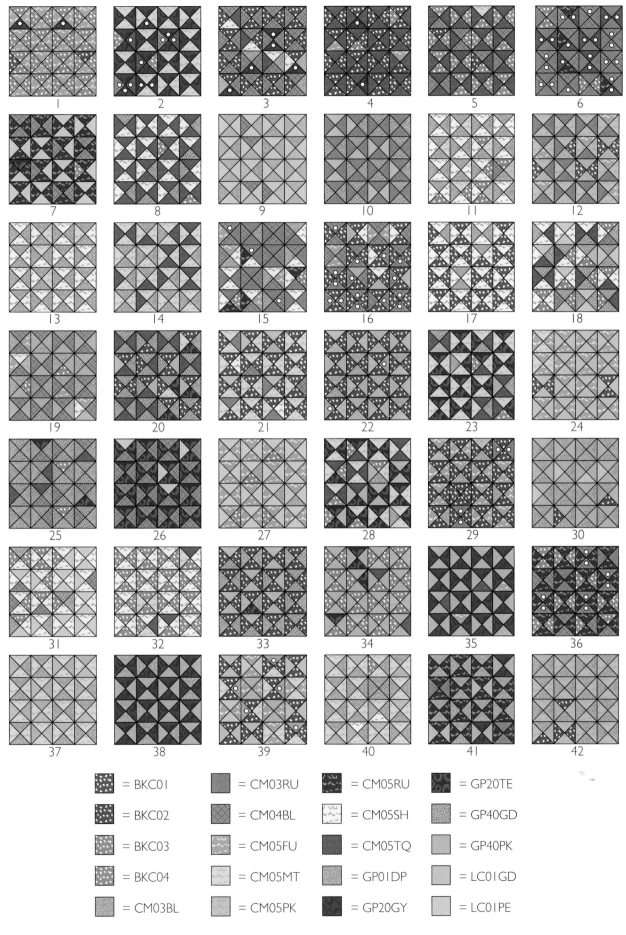

Patches marked with a white circle = WRONG SIDE of fabric used.

Quilt Assembly Diagram

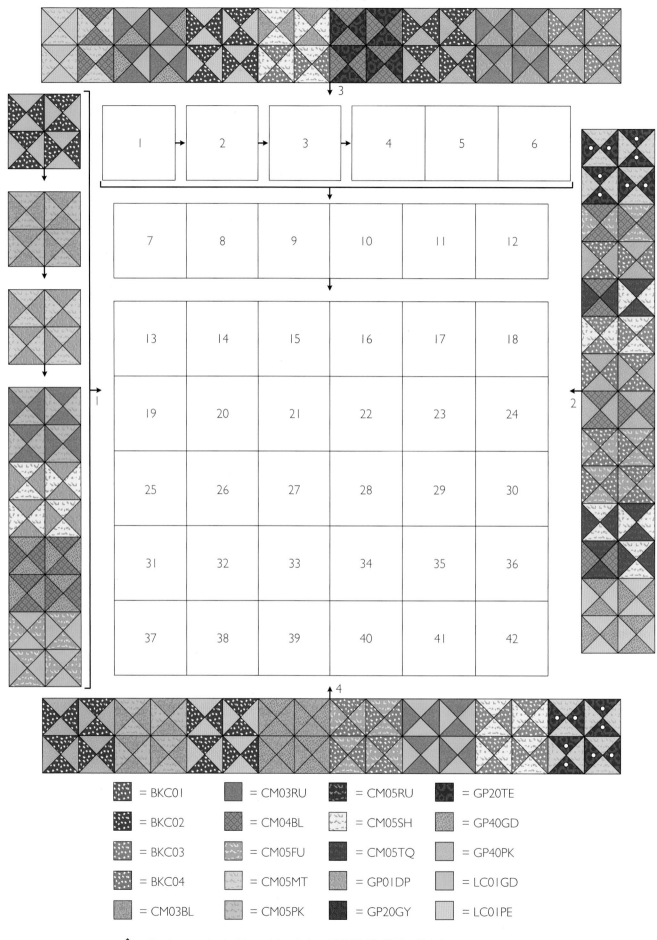

= BKC01   = CM03RU   = CM05RU   = GP20TE

= BKC02   = CM04BL   = CM05SH   = GP40GD

= BKC03   = CM05FU   = CM05TQ   = GP40PK

= BKC04   = CM05MT   = GP01DP   = LC01GD

= CM03BL   = CM05PK   = GP20GY   = LC01PE

Patches marked with a white circle = WRONG SIDE of fabric used.

Hazy Corners Quilt ★★

LIZA PRIOR-LUCY

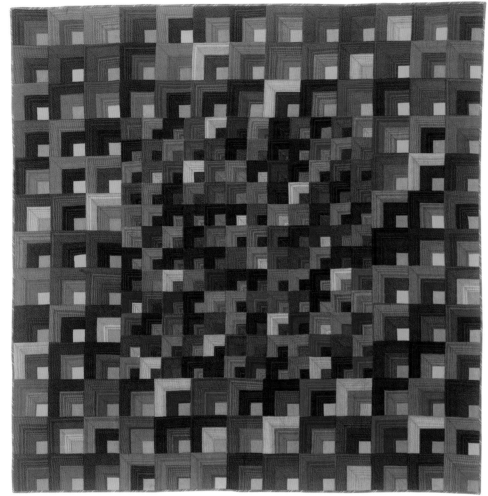

Scarlet	HZS18: ½ yd (45cm)
Pine	HZS19: ½ yd (45cm)
Aegean	HZS20: ½ yd (45cm)
Ginger	HZS21: ½ yd (45cm)
Grape	HZS22: ½ yd (45cm)

SHOT COTTON

Chartreuse	SC12: ¼ yd (25cm)
Mustard	SC16: ¼ yd (25cm)
Tobacco	SC18: ⅜ yd (35cm)

Backing Fabric: 5 yds (4.6m)
Any of the Woven Haze Stripes used in the quilt would be suitable for backing.

Binding:
WOVEN HAZE STRIPE
Terracotta   HZS10: ¾ yd (70cm)

Batting:
86in x 86in (218.5cm x 218.5cm).

Quilting thread:
Toning machine quilting thread.

Templates:
see pages 107, 118

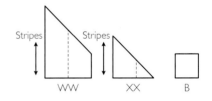

PATCH SHAPES
To achieve perfect mitred blocks a clever method is used. Striped fabrics are cut along the length of the fabric into strips and stitched in pairs to make rectangles. These are folded at the centre. The fold is removed and 2 pairs of patch shapes are cut using templates WW and XX. The blocks are stitched along the diagonal. A square patch shape (Template B) is inserted to complete the large blocks. The small blocks are pieced to form the quilt centre and the large blocks form the outside edges of the quilt. We have drawn Liza's quilt accurately, but this is meant to be an adventure, choose your own fabric combinations and give this quilt your own look.

CUTTING OUT
Template B: Cut 2½in (6.5cm) wide strips

One of the most popular quilts Kaffe and I ever made was Handkerchief Corners in our book, 'Passionate Patchwork'. The stripes used in that quilt were the original fabrics that Kaffe had woven with the help of the Oxfam organization. After a very nice run of almost 10 years, it was decided it was time to retire these old gems and bring to market a new collection of handwoven stripes. The Haze collection features Kaffe's quirky and brilliant colour combos in a new, more subtle way. I thought it would be good to try them out in this favourite pattern and here is the quilt. I am very pleased with this new, updated, Handkerchief Corners.

SIZE OF QUILT
The finished quilt will measure approx.
78in x 78in (198cm x 198cm).

MATERIALS
Patchwork Fabrics:
WOVEN HAZE STRIPE

Persimmon	HZS01: ½ yd (45cm)
Mustard	HZS02: ½ yd (45cm)
Cobalt	HZS03: ½ yd (45cm)
Pewter	HZS05: ½ yd (45cm)
Burgundy	HZS11: ½ yd (45cm)
Raspberry	HZS12: ½ yd (45cm)
Navy	HZS13: ½ yd (45cm)
Purple	HZS14: ½ yd (45cm)
Denim Blue	HZS15: ½ yd (45cm)
Green	HZS16: ½ yd (45cm)
Lavender	HZS17: ½ yd (45cm)

Cutting Diagrams

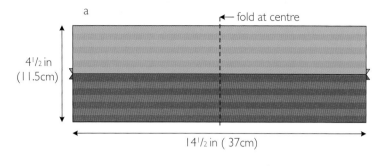

a

4½ in
(11.5cm)

← fold at centre

14½ in (37cm)

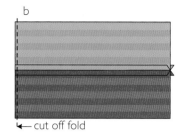

b

← cut off fold

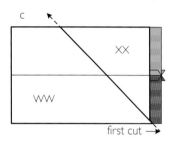

c

XX

WW

first cut →

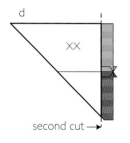

d

XX

second cut →

Large Block Assembly

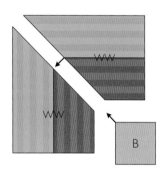

WW

WW

B

Small Block Assembly

XX

XX

across the width of the fabric. Each strip will give you 16 patches per 45in (114cm) wide fabric. Cut 63 in SC18, 35 in SC16 and 22 in SC12. Total 120 patches.

Templates WW and XX: From the WOVEN HAZE STRIPE fabrics cut 240 strips 2½in x 14½in (6.5cm x 36.75cm) along the length of the fabric, so that the stripes run along the length of the strip, then cut 24 strips 2½in x 9½in (6.5cm x 24.25cm) along the length of the fabric.

Binding: Cut 9yds (8.2m) of 2½in (6.5cm) wide bias binding in HZS10.

Backing: Cut 2 pieces 44in x 86in (112cm x 218.5cm) in backing fabric.

MAKING THE BLOCKS
Use a ¼in (6mm) seam allowance

throughout. Join 2 different 14½in (36.75cm) strips along the long edges as shown in diagram a. Open out and press. Join all the other 14½in (36.75cm) strips in the same way to make a total of 120 long joined strips. Then join the 9½in (24.25cm) strips in the same way to make 12 short joined strips.

Fold a 14½in (36.75cm) joined strip in half as shown in diagram b. Cut off the fold about ⅛in (3mm) from the crease and discard. So that the two layers of fabric remain perfectly aligned DO NOT separate or move them. Keeping the two layers of fabric together, cut the template WW patches as shown in diagram c. Remove the matching pair of template WW patch shapes very carefully (keeping them right sides together and aligned, as they will be stitched like this). Do not disturb the remaining fabric. Cut the

template XX patch shapes as shown in diagram d, again keeping the pair of patches together. Cut a total of 120 pairs of matching template WW and XX patches in this way from the 14½in (36.75cm) long joined strips.

An additional 24 pairs of template XX patches are required for the quilt centre. Cut these from the 9½in (24.25cm) short joined strips. Use the same method as before, folding the strips in half, remove the fold then cutting the matched pairs of template XX patches, but this time cut two pairs of patches from each folded strip.

For the 144 small blocks simply stitch each pair of template XX patches along the cut diagonal as shown in the small block assembly diagram.

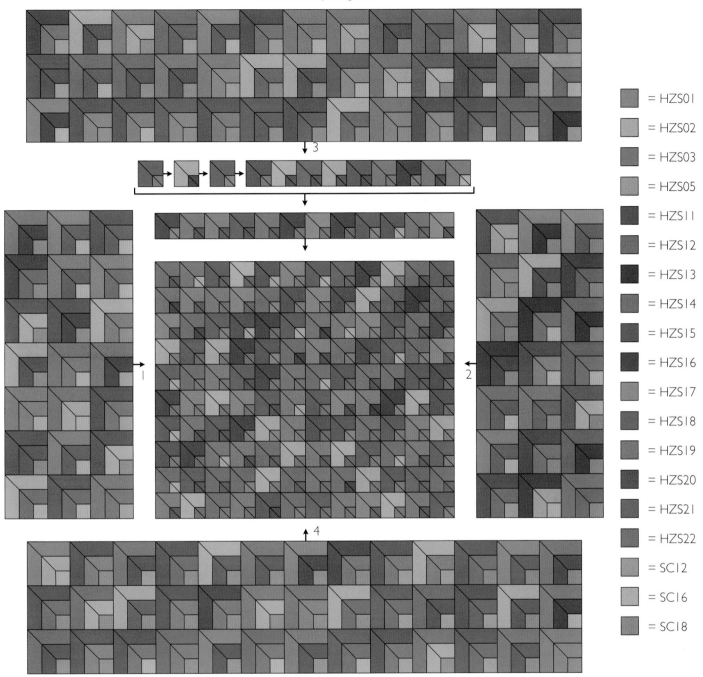

= HZS01
= HZS02
= HZS03
= HZS05
= HZS11
= HZS12
= HZS13
= HZS14
= HZS15
= HZS16
= HZS17
= HZS18
= HZS19
= HZS20
= HZS21
= HZS22
= SC12
= SC16
= SC18

For the 120 large blocks stitch each pair of template WW patches along the cut diagonal. Then using the inset seam method (see Patchwork Know How page 120) join a template B square into each block as shown in the large block assembly diagram.

MAKING THE QUILT
Piece the small blocks into 12 rows of 12 blocks with the blocks all facing in the same direction as shown in the quilt assembly

diagram. Join the rows to form the quilt centre. Piece the large blocks into two 3 x 7 block sections for the sides of the quilt and two 3 x 13 block sections for the top and bottom of the quilt, again with the blocks all facing in the same direction. Join the sections to the quilt centre as indicated in the quilt assembly diagram.

FINISHING THE QUILT
Press the quilt top. Seam the backing pieces

using a ¼in (6mm) seam allowance to form a piece approx. 86in x 86in (218.5cm x 218.5cm). Layer the quilt top, batting and backing and baste together (see page 122). Use toning machine quilting thread. In the centre section quilt in the ditch around the outside of the small blocks and along the diagonal seams. Quilt in the ditch along all the patch seams in the large blocks. Trim the quilt edges and attach the binding (see page 122).

Moonflowers Quilt ★★

RUTH EGLINTON

I originally chose pinks and blues for this little 'scrap' style quilt, but after making up sample blocks I swapped in Plumeria Yellow for the pink version and suddenly the quilt came alive. The arrangement of colours and fabrics is really up to you, but I like to gather the colours in 'pools' and then link them with the checkerboard sections.

SIZE OF QUILT
The finished quilt will measure approx.
46in x 34½in (117cm x 88cm).

MATERIALS
Patchwork Fabrics:
PAPERWEIGHT
Sludge   GP20SL: ⅜ yd (35cm)
LEAVES
Periwinkle   GP30PE: ⅜ yd (35cm)
PAISLEY STRIPE
Blue   GP32BL: ⅜ yd (35cm)
SPOOLS
Lavender   GP34LV: ¼ yd (25cm)
EMBROIDERED LEAF
Pink   GP42PK: ¼ yd (25cm)
CAMOUFLAGE
Pearl   GP44PR: ⅛ yd (15cm)
VEGETABLE LEAVES
Purple   MN05PU: ¼ yd (25cm)
DAHLIA
Blue   MN06BL: ¼ yd (25cm)
Pink   MN06PK: ¼ yd (25cm)
Purple   MN06PU: ¼ yd (25cm)
MARIGOLD
Purple   MN07PU: ⅛ yd (15cm)
PLUMERIA
Blue   MN10BL: ⅛ yd (15cm)
Purple   MN10PU: ⅛ yd (15cm)
Yellow   MN10YE: ⅛ yd (15cm)
SHOT COTTON
Jade   SC41: ¼ yd (25cm)
Lime   SC43: ½ yd (45cm)
                  includes binding.
Mist   SC48: ⅝ yd (60cm)

Backing Fabric: 1½ yds (1.4m)
Any of the Shot Cotton fabrics listed above would be suitable for backing.

Binding:
SHOT COTTON
Lime   SC43: see patchwork fabrics

Batting:
52in x 40in (132cm x 102cm).

Quilting thread:
Soft blue hand quilting thread.

a

Templates:
see pages 107, 115

A   B   C   D   E   Large Triangle

PATCH SHAPES
Star blocks made using 2 square patch shapes (Templates A & B) and 2 triangle patch shapes (Templates C, D) are then set 'on point' using a third triangle patch shape (Large Triangle, cut to size). These star blocks are trimmed to size and interspaced with checkerboard sections made up from a third square patch shape (Template E). There is also a panel with hand appliqué, the appliqué shapes are on page 115.

CUTTING OUT
Large Triangles: Cut two 11in (28cm) squares from GP20SL, GP30PE and GP32BL (total 6 squares). Cut each square twice diagonally to make 4 triangles. Note: do not move the patches until both diagonals have been cut. Total 24 Large triangles. These triangles are cut oversize and trimmed later. Reserve remaining GP32BL fabric for Template D.
Template A: Cut 4½in (11.5cm) wide strip across the width of the fabric. Cut 1 in GP34LV, GP42PK, MN05PU, MN06BL, MN06PK and MN06PU. Reserve leftover strip and trim for template E.
Template B: Cut 2½in (6.5cm) wide strips across the width of the fabric. Each strip will give you 16 patches per 45in (114cm) wide fabric. Cut 24 in SC48.
Template C: Cut 5¼in (13.5cm) wide strips across the width of the fabric. Each strip will give you 32 patches per 45in (114cm) wide fabric. Cut 6 × 5¼in (13.5cm) squares, then cut each square twice diagonally to make 4 triangles. This will ensure the long side of the triangle will not have a bias edge. Cut 24 in SC48.
Template E: Cut 3⅜in (8.5cm) wide strips across the width of the fabric. Cut 10 in MN06BL, 8 in GP34LV, GP44PR, MN10PU, SC41, SC48, 6 in MN07PU, MN10YE, 4 in MN05PU, MN10BL, SC43, 2 in GP42PK, MN06PK and MN06PU. Reserve leftover strip and trim for template D.
Template D: Cut 2⅞in (7.25cm) wide strips across the width of the fabric. Cut 8 in GP32BL, GP44PR, MN07PU, MN10BL,

MN10PU and MN10YE.
Appliqué Panel: Cut 1 rectangle 6¾in × 24in. This is oversize and will be trimmed when the hand appliqué is complete.
Appliqué Shapes: Note: The appliqué shapes do not include a seam allowance. Cut 4 leaf shapes in SC43, 4 oval flower shapes in MN06PU, 4 circle flower centres in MN10YE. **Appliqué Vine:** Cut 19in (48cm) of bias strip 1¼in (3.25cm) wide in SC41.

Binding: Cut 4 strips 2½in (6.5cm) wide × width of fabric in SC43.

Backing: Cut 1 piece 52in × 40in (132cm × 102cm) in backing fabric.

MAKING THE BLOCKS
Use a ¼in (6mm) seam allowance throughout. Piece 6 star blocks following block assembly diagrams a, b and c. Trim the finished blocks evenly to 12in square to the raw edge. Piece the checkerboard sections following block assembly diagram d.

MAKING THE APPLIQUÉ PANEL
Find the centre of the background panel and mark with a washable marker. Mark the position of the curved stem, leaves and flowers using the Appliqué shapes pattern on page 115. The pattern is for half the design, rotate on the dotted line to complete. Appliqué the curved stem. (See the Hand Appliqué Section in Patchwork Know How page 120). Appliqué the flowers and leaves into place. Press lightly and trim the panel evenly to 23½in × 6¼in to the raw edge.

MAKING THE QUILT
Piece the various blocks together as indicated in the quilt assembly diagram.

FINISHING THE QUILT
Press the quilt top. Layer the quilt top, batting and backing and baste together (see page 122). Starting at the appliqué section echo quilt around the appliqué shapes using soft blue hand quilting thread. Work the quilting in lines between ¼ and 1¼ inches (0.6cm to 3cm) apart working out and introducing additional shapes as you like. Ruth used the appliqué leaf shape placed in trios to add interest to the quilting design. Trim the quilt edges and attach the binding (see page 122).

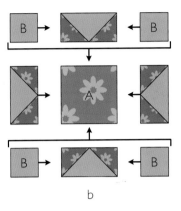

b

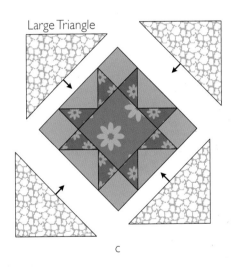

Large Triangle

c

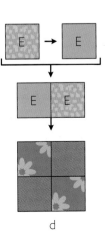

d

Quilt Assembly Diagram

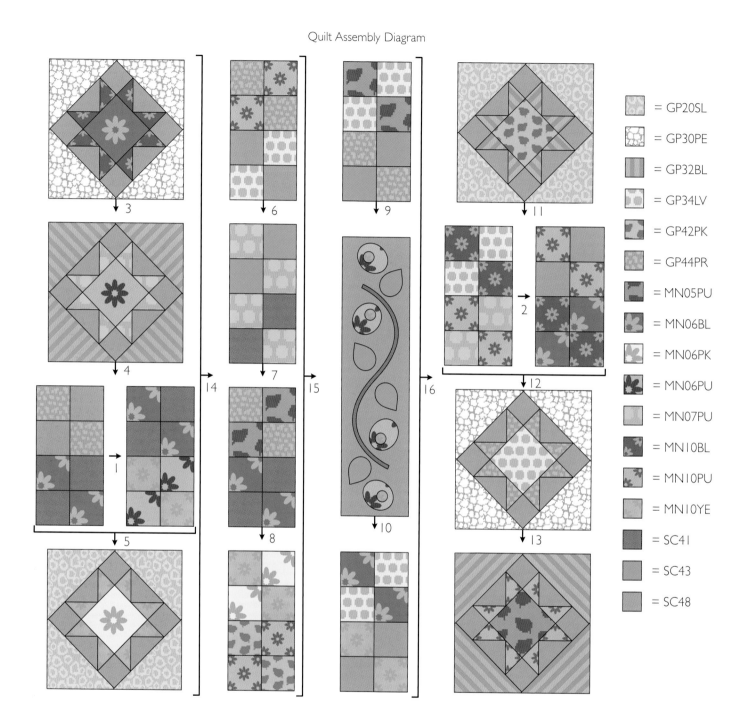

= GP20SL
= GP30PE
= GP32BL
= GP34LV
= GP42PK
= GP44PR
= MN05PU
= MN06BL
= MN06PK
= MN06PU
= MN07PU
= MN10BL
= MN10PU
= MN10YE
= SC41
= SC43
= SC48

Templates

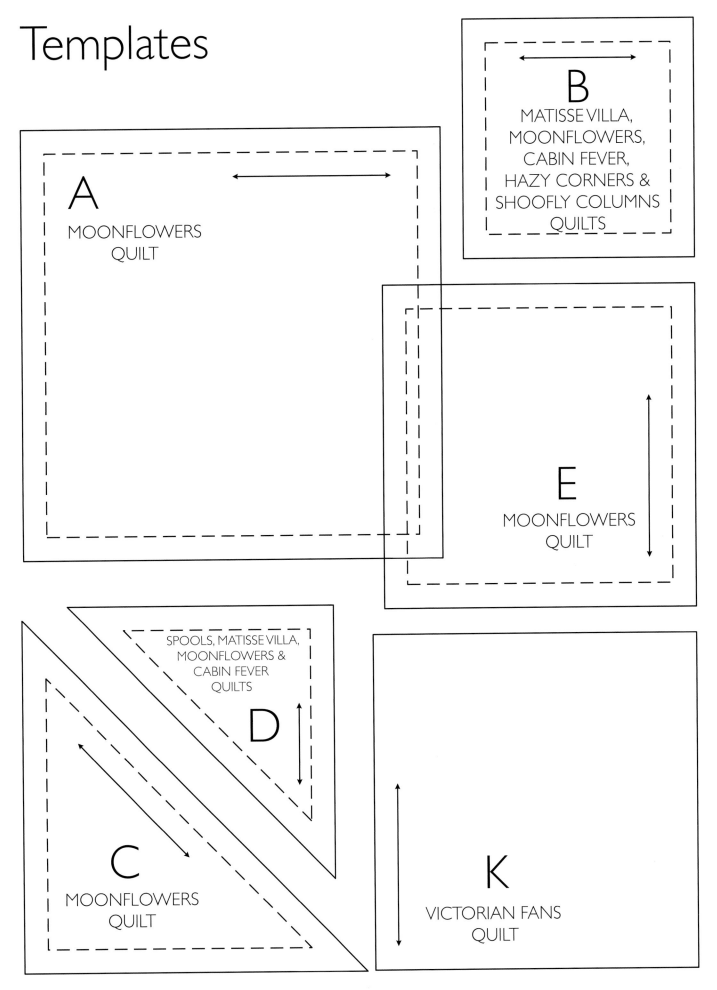

A
MOONFLOWERS
QUILT

B
MATISSE VILLA,
MOONFLOWERS,
CABIN FEVER,
HAZY CORNERS &
SHOOFLY COLUMNS
QUILTS

E
MOONFLOWERS
QUILT

D
SPOOLS, MATISSE VILLA,
MOONFLOWERS &
CABIN FEVER
QUILTS

C
MOONFLOWERS
QUILT

K
VICTORIAN FANS
QUILT

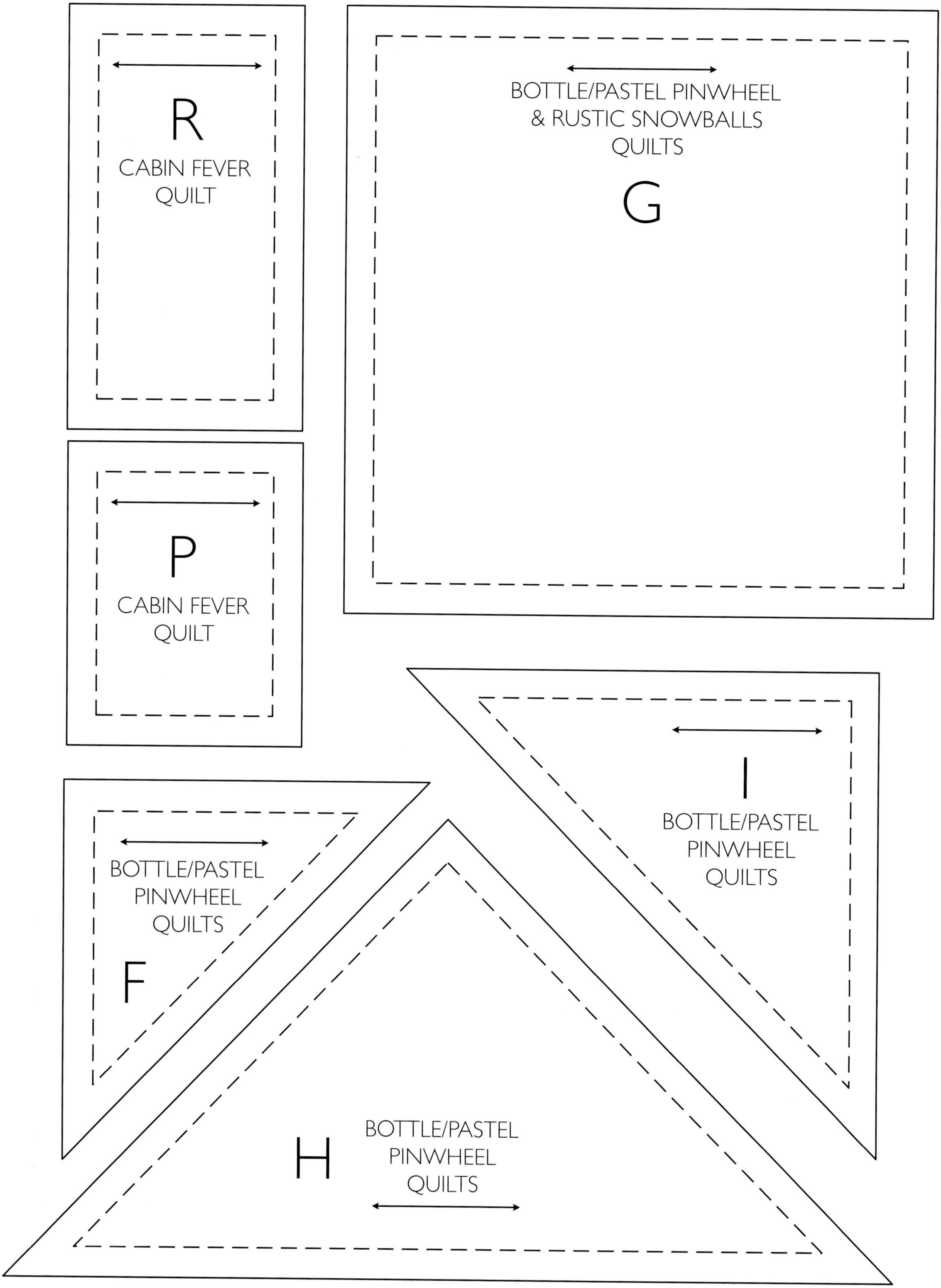

R

CABIN FEVER
QUILT

BOTTLE/PASTEL PINWHEEL
& RUSTIC SNOWBALLS
QUILTS

G

P

CABIN FEVER
QUILT

I

BOTTLE/PASTEL
PINWHEEL
QUILTS

BOTTLE/PASTEL
PINWHEEL
QUILTS

F

BOTTLE/PASTEL
PINWHEEL
QUILTS

H

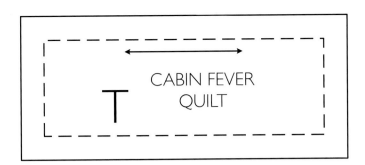

T CABIN FEVER QUILT

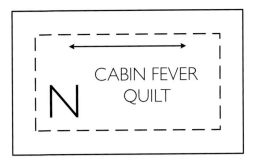

N CABIN FEVER QUILT

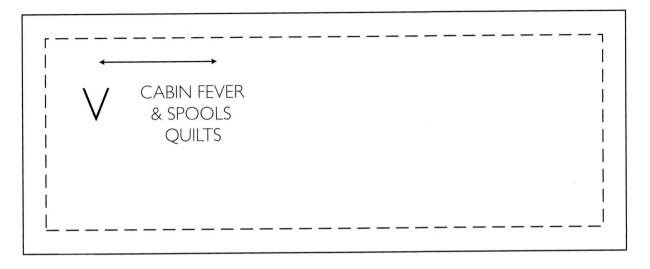

V CABIN FEVER & SPOOLS QUILTS

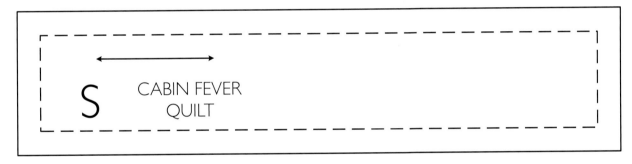

S CABIN FEVER QUILT

Q CABIN FEVER QUILT

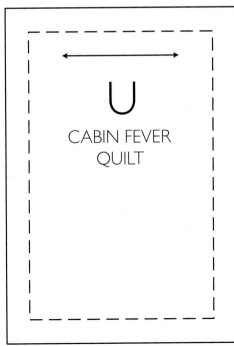

U CABIN FEVER QUILT

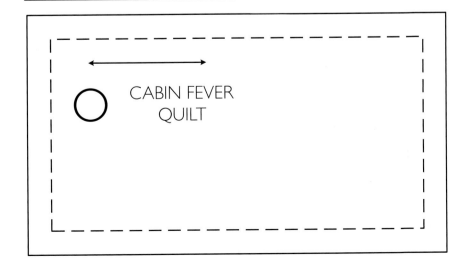

O CABIN FEVER QUILT

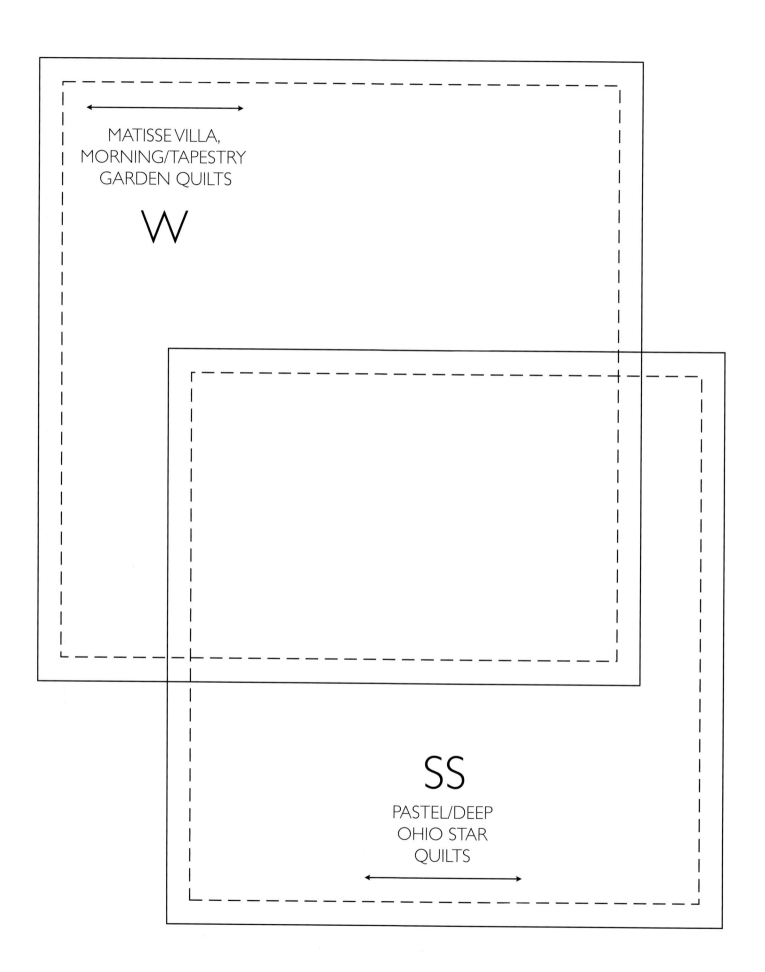

MATISSE VILLA,
MORNING/TAPESTRY
GARDEN QUILTS

W

SS

PASTEL/DEEP
OHIO STAR
QUILTS

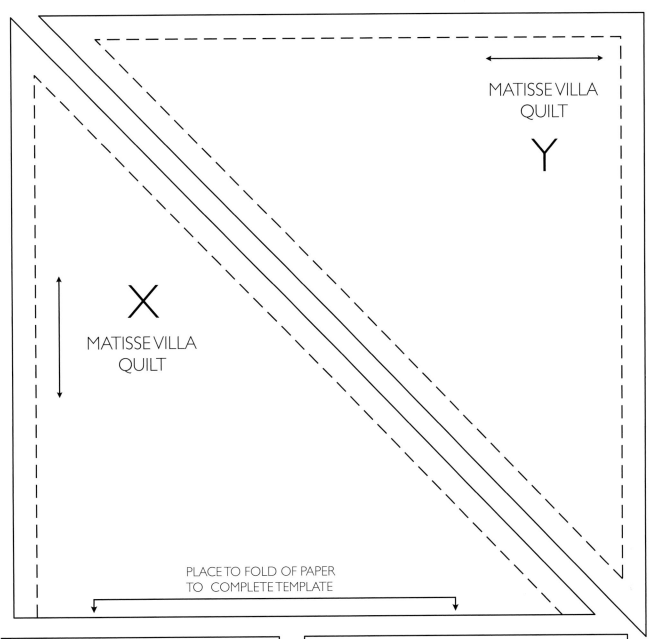

MATISSE VILLA
QUILT

Y

X

MATISSE VILLA
QUILT

PLACE TO FOLD OF PAPER
TO COMPLETE TEMPLATE

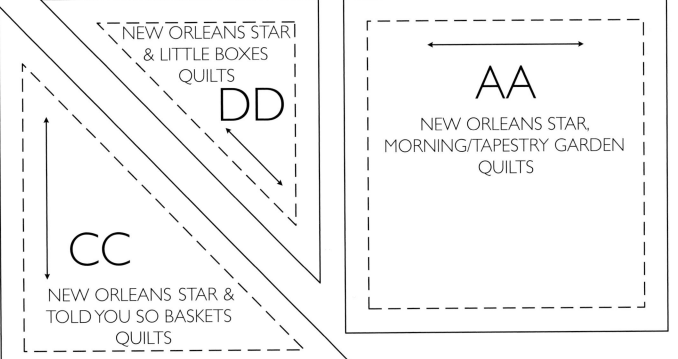

NEW ORLEANS STAR
& LITTLE BOXES
QUILTS

DD

AA

NEW ORLEANS STAR,
MORNING/TAPESTRY GARDEN
QUILTS

CC

NEW ORLEANS STAR &
TOLD YOU SO BASKETS
QUILTS

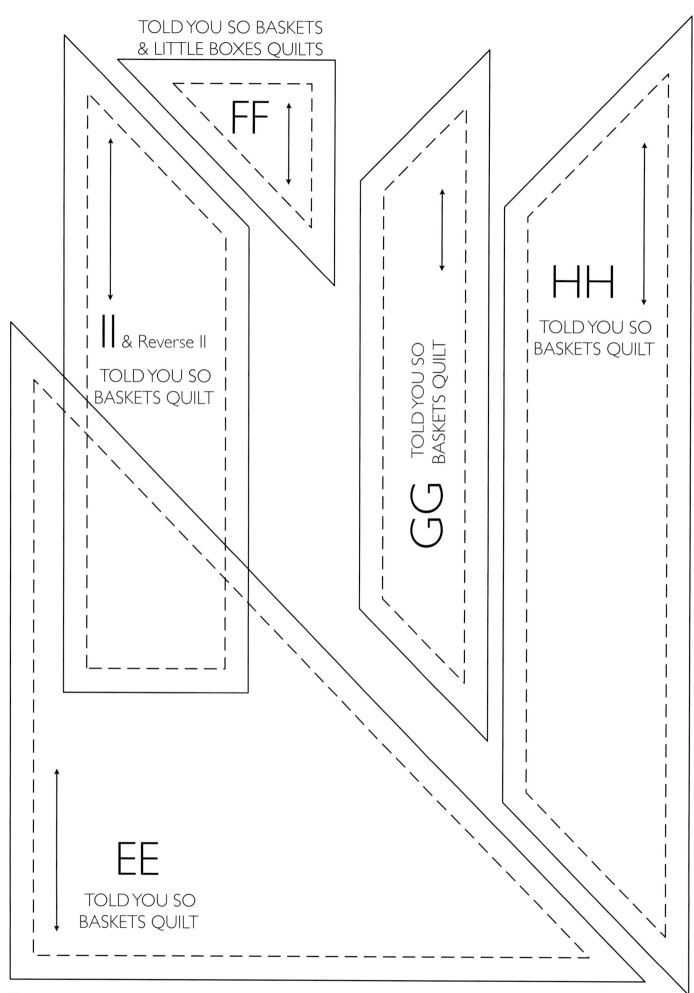

TOLD YOU SO BASKETS
& LITTLE BOXES QUILTS

FF

II & Reverse II

TOLD YOU SO
BASKETS QUILT

GG TOLD YOU SO
BASKETS QUILT

HH

TOLD YOU SO
BASKETS QUILT

EE

TOLD YOU SO
BASKETS QUILT

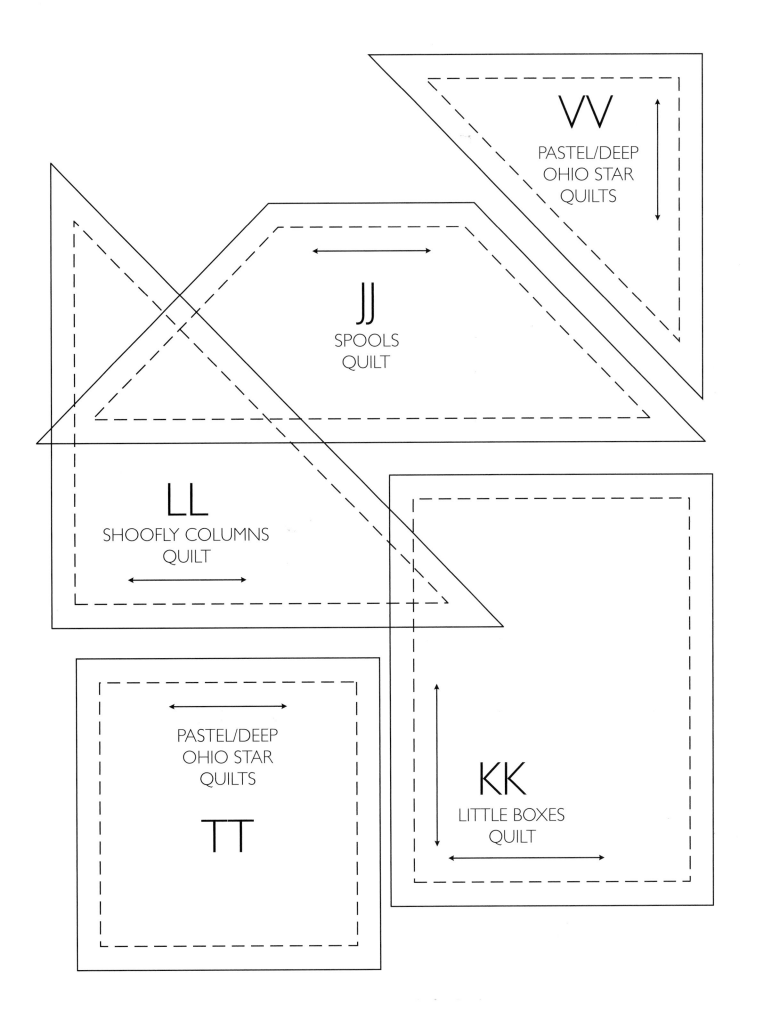

VV

PASTEL/DEEP
OHIO STAR
QUILTS

JJ
SPOOLS
QUILT

LL
SHOOFLY COLUMNS
QUILT

KK
LITTLE BOXES
QUILT

PASTEL/DEEP
OHIO STAR
QUILTS

TT

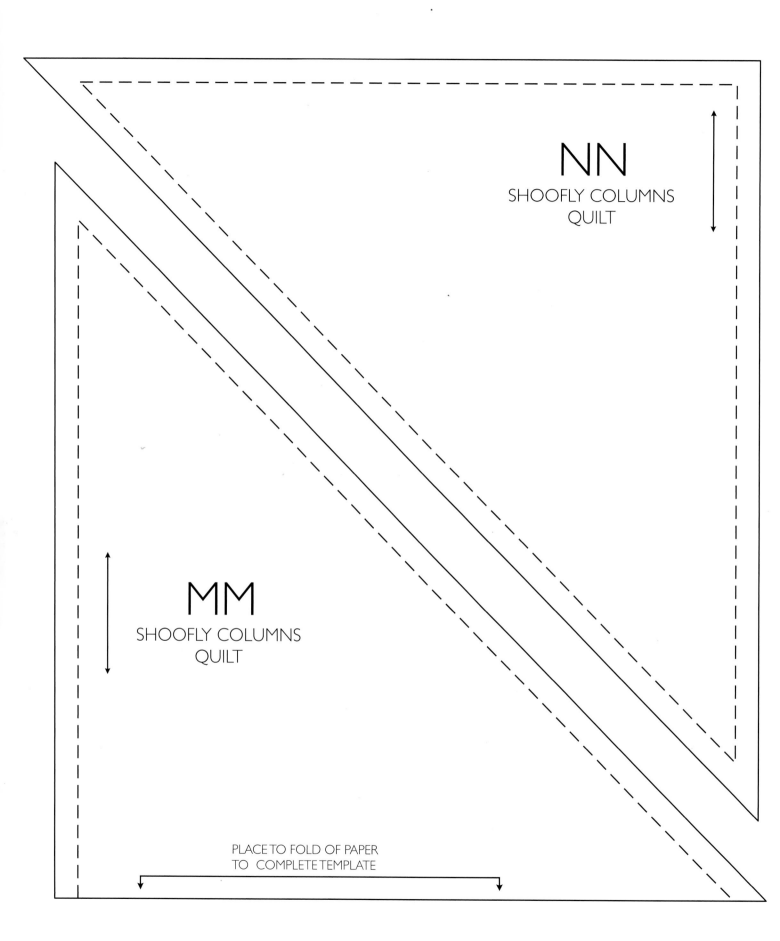

NN
SHOOFLY COLUMNS
QUILT

MM
SHOOFLY COLUMNS
QUILT

PLACE TO FOLD OF PAPER
TO COMPLETE TEMPLATE

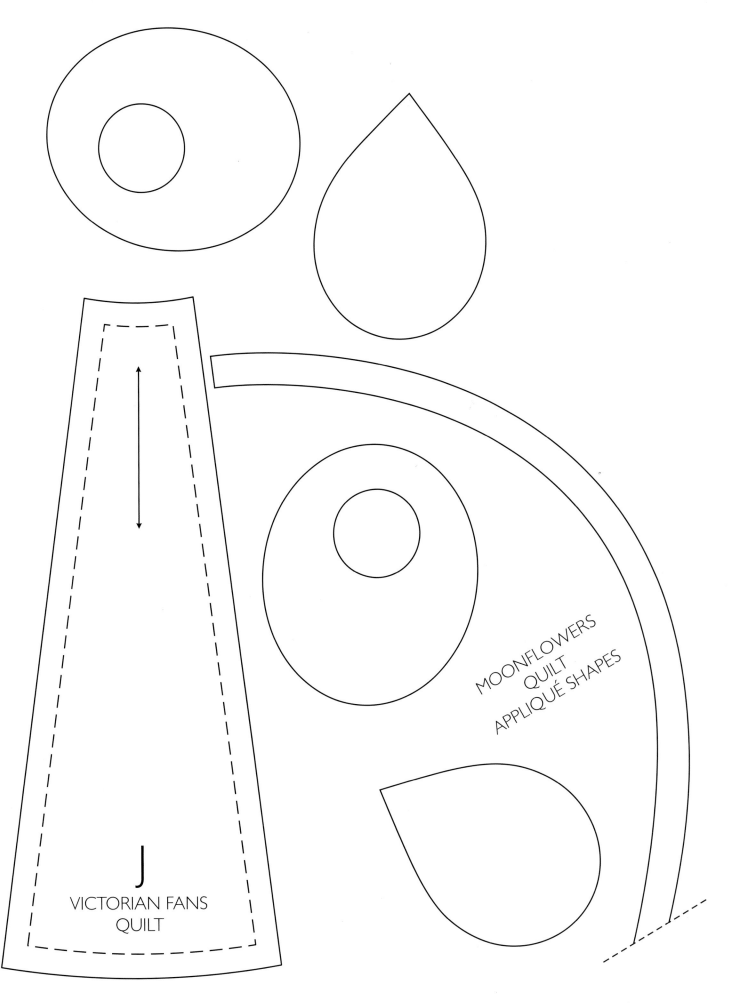

J
VICTORIAN FANS
QUILT

MOONFLOWERS
QUILT
APPLIQUÉ SHAPES

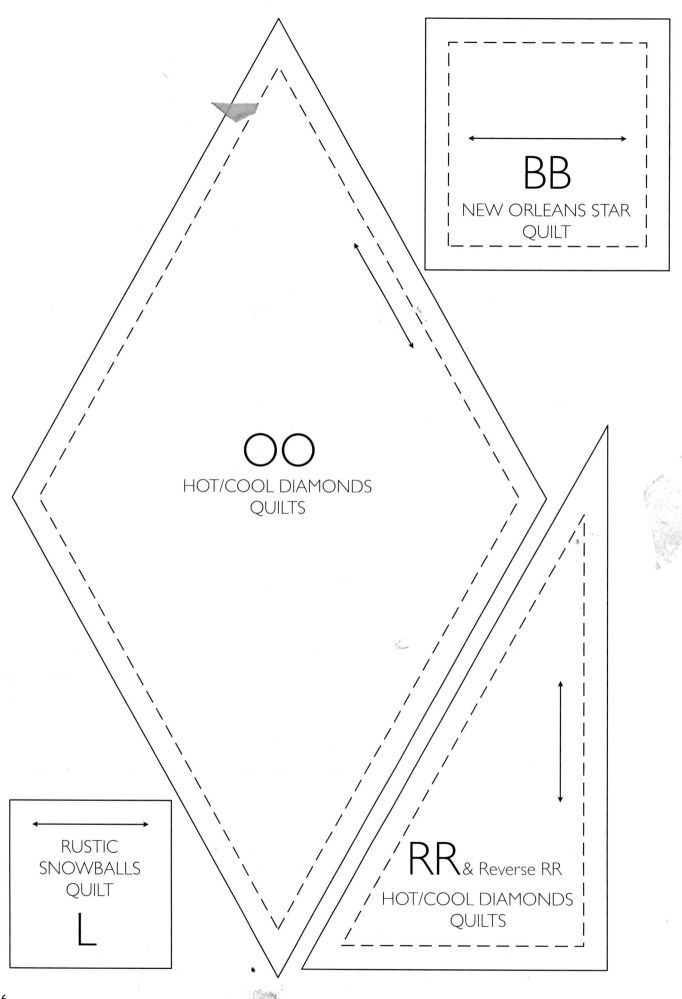

OO
HOT/COOL DIAMONDS
QUILTS

BB
NEW ORLEANS STAR
QUILT

RR & Reverse RR
HOT/COOL DIAMONDS
QUILTS

RUSTIC
SNOWBALLS
QUILT

L

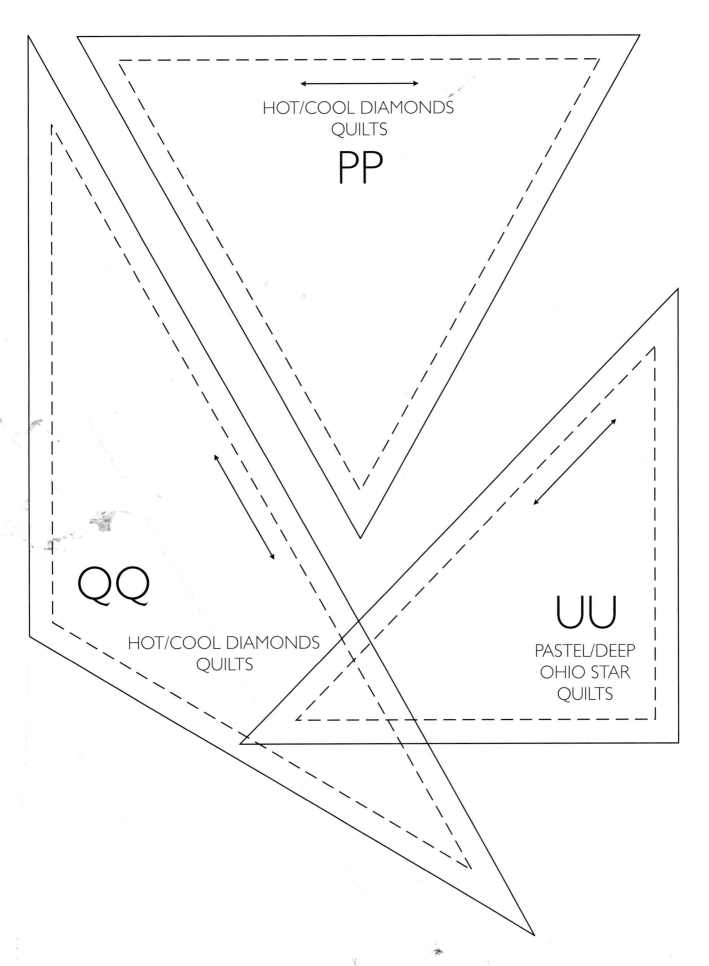

HOT/COOL DIAMONDS
QUILTS

PP

QQ

HOT/COOL DIAMONDS
QUILTS

UU

PASTEL/DEEP
OHIO STAR
QUILTS

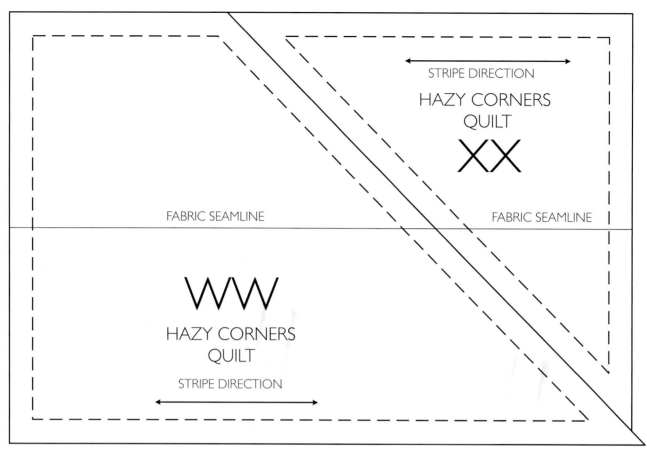

STRIPE DIRECTION

HAZY CORNERS
QUILT

XX

FABRIC SEAMLINE

FABRIC SEAMLINE

WW

HAZY CORNERS
QUILT

STRIPE DIRECTION

Z

NEW ORLEANS STAR
QUILT

Patchwork Know How

These instructions are intended for the novice quilt maker, providing the basic information needed to make the projects in this book, along with some useful tips.

Preparing the fabric

Prewash all new fabrics before you begin, to ensure that there will be no uneven shrinkage and no bleeding of colours when the quilt is laundered. Press the fabric whilst it is still damp to return crispness to it.

Making templates

Transparent template plastic is the best material, it is durable and allows you to see the fabric and select certain motifs. You can also use thin stiff cardboard.

Templates for machine piecing

1 Trace off the actual-sized template provided either directly on to template plastic, or tracing paper, and then on to thin cardboard. Use a ruler to help you trace off the straight cutting line, dotted seam line and grainlines. Some of the templates in this book are so large that we have only been able to give you half of them. Before transferring them on to plastic or card, trace off the half template, place the fold edge up to the fold of a piece of paper, and carefully draw around the shape. Cut out the paper double thickness, and open out for the completed template.

2 Cut out the traced off template using a craft knife, ruler and a self-healing cutting mat.

3 Punch holes in the corners of the template, at each point on the seam line, using a hole punch.

Templates for hand piecing

• Make a template as for machine piecing, but do not trace off the cutting line. Use the dotted seam line as the outer edge of the template.

• This template allows you to draw the seam lines directly on to the fabric. The seam allowances can then be cut by eye around the patch.

Cutting the fabric

On the individual instructions for each patchwork, you will find a summary of all the patch shapes used.
Always mark and cut out any border and binding strips first, followed by the largest patch shapes and finally the smallest ones, to make the most efficient use of your fabric. The border and binding strips are best cut using a rotary cutter.

Rotary cutting

Rotary cut strips are usually cut across the fabric from selvedge to selvedge, but some projects may vary, so please read through all the instructions before you start cutting the fabrics.

1 Before beginning to cut, press out any folds or creases in the fabric. If you are cutting a large piece of fabric, you will need to fold it several times to fit the cutting mat. When there is only a single fold, place the fold facing you. If the fabric is too wide to be folded only once, fold it concertina-style until it fits your mat. A small rotary cutter with a sharp blade will cut up to 6 layers of fabric; a large cutter up to 8 layers.

2 To ensure that your cut strips are straight and even, the folds must be placed exactly parallel to the straight edges of the fabric and along a line on the cutting mat.

3 Place a plastic ruler over the raw edge of the fabric, overlapping it about ½in (1.25cm). Make sure that the ruler is at right angles to both the straight edges and the fold to ensure that you cut along the straight grain. Press down on the ruler and wheel the cutter away from yourself along the edge of the ruler.

4 Open out the fabric to check the edge. Don't worry if it's not perfectly straight; a little wiggle will not show when the quilt is stitched together. Re-fold fabric, then place the ruler over the trimmed edge, aligning edge with the markings on the ruler that match the correct strip width. Cut strip along the edge of the ruler.

Using templates

The most efficient way to cut out templates is by first rotary cutting a strip of fabric the width stated for your template, and then marking off your templates along the strip, edge to edge at

the required angle. This method leaves hardly any waste and gives a random effect to your patches.
A less efficient method is to fussy cut, where the templates are cut individually by placing them on particular motifs or stripes, to create special effects. Although this method is more wasteful it yields very interesting results.

1 Place the template face down on the wrong side of the fabric, with the grain line arrow following the straight grain of the fabric, if indicated. Be careful though - check with your individual instructions, as some instructions may ask you to cut patches on varying grains.

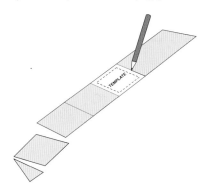

2 Hold the template firmly in place and draw around it with a sharp pencil or crayon, marking in the corner dots or seam lines. To save fabric, position patches close together or even touching. Don't worry if outlines positioned on the straight grain when drawn on striped fabrics do not always match the stripes when cut - this will add a degree of visual excitement to the patchwork!

3 Once you've drawn all the pieces needed, you are ready to cut the fabric, with either a rotary cutter and ruler, or a pair of sharp sewing scissors.

Basic hand and machine piecing

Patches can be joined together by hand or machine. Machine stitching is quicker, but hand assembly allows you to carry your patches around with you and work on them in every spare moment. The choice is yours. For techniques that are new to you, practise on scrap pieces of fabric until you feel confident.

Machine piecing

Follow the quilt instructions for the order in which to piece the individual patchwork blocks and then assemble the blocks together in rows.

1 Seam lines are not marked on the fabric, so stitch ¼in (6mm) seams using the machine needle plate, a ¼in (6mm) wide machine foot, or tape stuck to the machine as a guide. Pin two patches with right sides together, matching edges.

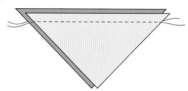

Set your machine at 10-12 stitches per inch (2.5cm) and stitch seams from edge to edge, removing pins as you feed the fabric through the machine.

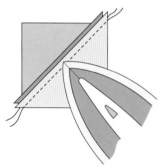

2 Press the seams of each patchwork block to one side before attempting to join it to another block.

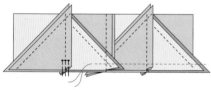

3 When joining rows of blocks, make sure that adjacent seam allowances are pressed in opposite directions to reduce bulk and make matching easier. Pin pieces together directly through the stitch line and to the right and left of the seam. Remove pins as you sew. Continue pressing seams to one side as you work.

Hand piecing

1 Pin two patches with right sides together, so that the marked seam lines are facing outwards.

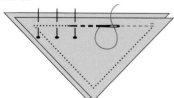

2 Using a single strand of strong thread, secure the corner of a seam line with a couple of back stitches.

3 Sew running stitches along the marked line, working 8-10 stitches per inch (2.5cm) and ending at the opposite seam line corner with a few back stitches. When hand piecing never stitch over the seam allowances.

4 Press the seams to one side, as shown in machine piecing (Step 2).

Inset seams.

In some patchwork layouts a patch will have to be sewn into an angled corner formed by the joining of two other patches. Use the following method whether you are machine or hand piecing. Don't be intimidated - this is not hard to do once you have learned a couple of techniques. The seam is sewn from the centre outwards in two halves to ensure that no tucks appear at the centre.

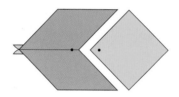

1 Mark with dots exactly where the inset will be joined and mark the seam lines on the wrong side of the fabric on the inset patch.

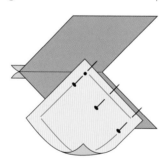

2 With right sides together and inset piece on top, pin through the dots to match the inset points. Pin the rest of the seam at right angles to the stitching line, along one edge of an adjoining patch.

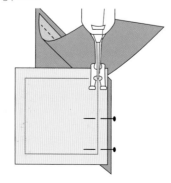

3 Stitch the patch in place along the seam line starting with the needle down through the inset point dots. Secure thread with a backstitch if hand piecing, or stitch forward for a few stitches before backstitching, when machine piecing.

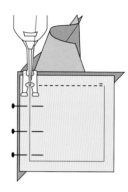

4 Pivot the patch, to enable it to align with the adjacent side of the angled corner, allowing you work on the second half of the seam. Starting with a pin at the inset point once again. Pin and stitch the second side in place, as before. Check seams and press carefully.

Hand appliqué

Good preparation is essential for speedy and accurate hand appliqué. The finger-pressing method is suitable for needle-turning application, used for simple shapes like leaves and flowers. Using a card template is the best method for bold simple motifs such as circles.

Finger-pressing:

1 To make your template, transfer the appliqué design on to stiff card using carbon paper, and cut out template. Trace around the outline of your appliquéd shape on to the right side of your fabric using a well sharpened pencil. Cut out shapes, adding a ¼in (6mm) seam allowance all around by eye.

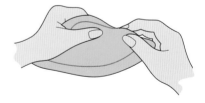

2 Hold shape right side up and fold under the seam, turning along your drawn line, pinch to form a crease. Dampening the fabric makes this very easy. When using shapes with 'points' such as leaves turn the seam allowance at the 'point' in first as shown in the diagram, then continue all round the shape. If your shapes have sharp curves you can snip the seam allowance to ease the curve. Take care not to stretch the appliqué shapes as you work.

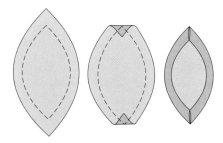

Card templates:

1 Cut out appliqué shapes as shown in step 1 of finger-pressing. Make a circular template from thin cardboard, without seam allowances.

2 Using a matching thread, work a row of running stitches close to the edge of the fabric circle. Place thin cardboard template in the centre of the fabric circle on the wrong side of the fabric.

3 Carefully pull up the running stitches to gather up the edge of the fabric circle around the cardboard template. Press, so that no puckers or tucks appear on the right side. Then, carefully pop out the cardboard template without distorting the fabric shape.

Bias Vines and Stems:

1 Bias cut strips of fabric twice the desired finished width of the vine plus ½in (12mm). Fold the strip right side out matching the raw edges carefully and gently press. Lay the strip along the desired path and ease curves. Stitch the vine in place ¼in (6mm) from the raw edge as shown in the diagram, this can be done by hand or machine.

2 Fold the free edge of the vine over to cover the raw edges, again easing the curves, and slipstitch in place using a thread matching the vine.

Needle-turning application

1 Take the appliqué shape and pin in position. Stroke the seam allowance under with the tip of the needle as far as the creased pencil line, and hold securely in place with your thumb. Using a matching thread, bring the needle up from the back of the block into the edge of the shape and proceed to blind-hem in place. This is a stitch where the motifs appear to be held on invisibly. Bring the thread out from below through the folded edge of the motif, never on the top. The stitches must be worked small, even and close together to prevent the seam allowance from unfolding and frayed edges appearing. Try to avoid pulling the stitches too tight, as this will cause the motifs to pucker up. Work around the whole shape, stroking under each small section before sewing.

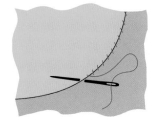

Quilting and finishing

When you have finished piecing your patchwork and added any borders, press it carefully. It is now ready for quilting.

Marking quilting designs and motifs

Many tools are available for marking quilting patterns, check the manufacturer's instructions for use and test on scraps of fabric from your project. Use an acrylic ruler for marking straight lines.

Stencils: Some designs require stencils, these can be made at home, by transferring the designs on to template plastic, or stiff cardboard. The design is then cut away in the form of long dashes, to act as guides for both internal and external lines. These stencils are a quick method for producing an identical set of repeated designs.

Preparing the backing and batting

• Remove the selvedges and piece together the backing fabric to form a backing at least 3in (7.5cm) larger all round than the patchwork top.

• For quilting choose a fairly thin batting, preferably pure cotton, to give your quilt a flat appearance. If your batting has been rolled up, unroll it and let it rest before cutting it to the same size as the backing.

• For a large quilt it may be necessary to join 2 pieces of batting to fit. Lay the pieces of batting on a flat surface so that they overlap by approx 8in (20cm). Cut a curved line through both layers.

2. Carefully peel away the two narrow pieces and discard. Butt the curved cut edges back together. Stitch the two pieces together using a large herringbone stitch.

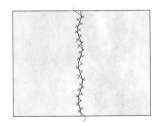

Basting the layers together

1 On a bare floor or large work surface, lay out the backing with wrong side uppermost. Use weights along the edges to keep it taut.

2 Lay the batting on the backing and smooth it out gently. Next lay the patchwork top, right side up, on top of the batting and smooth gently until there are no wrinkles. Pin at the corners and at the midpoints of each side, close to the edges.

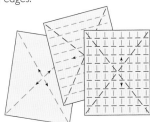

3 Beginning at the centre, baste diagonal lines outwards to the corners, making your

stitches about 3in (7.5cm) long. Then, again starting at the centre, baste horizontal and vertical lines out to the edges. Continue basting until you have basted a grid of lines about 4in (10cm) apart over the entire quilt.

4 For speed, when machine quilting, some quilters prefer to baste their quilt sandwich layers together using rust-proof safety pins, spaced at 4in (10cm) intervals over the entire quilt.

Hand quilting

This is best done with the quilt mounted on a quilting frame or hoop, but as long as you have basted the quilt well, a frame is not essential. With the quilt top facing upwards, begin at the centre of the quilt and make even running stitches following the design. It is more important to make even stitches on both sides of the quilt than to make small ones. Start and finish your stitching with back stitches and bury the ends of your threads in the batting.

Machine quilting

• For a flat looking quilt, always use a walking foot on your machine for straight lines, and a darning foot for free-motion quilting.

• It's best to start your quilting at the centre of the quilt and work out towards the borders, doing the straight quilting lines first (stitch-in-the-ditch) followed by the free-motion quilting.

• When free motion quilting stitch in a loose meandering style as shown in the diagrams. Do not stitch too closely as this will make the quilt feel stiff when finished. If you wish you can include floral themes or follow shapes on the printed fabrics for added interest.

• Make it easier for yourself by handling the quilt properly. Roll up the excess quilt neatly to

fit under your sewing machine arm, and use a table, or chair to help support the weight of the quilt that hangs down the other side.

Preparing to bind the edges

Once you have quilted or tied your quilt sandwich together, remove all the basting stitches. Then, baste around the outer edge of the quilt ¼in (6mm) from the edge of the top patchwork layer. Trim the back and batting to the edge of the patchwork and straighten the edge of the patchwork if necessary.

Making the binding

1 Cut bias or straight grain strips the width required for your binding, making sure the grainline is running the correct way on your straight grain strips. Cut enough strips until you have the required length to go around the edge of your quilt.

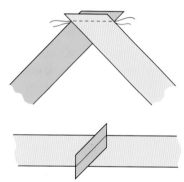

2 To join strips together, the two ends that are to be joined must be cut at a 45 degree angle, as above. Stitch right sides together, trim turnings and press seam open.

Binding the edges

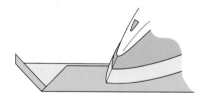

1 Cut starting end of binding strip at a 45-degree angle, fold a ¼in (6mm) turning to wrong side along cut edge and press in place. With wrong sides together, fold strip in half lengthways, keeping raw edges level, and press.

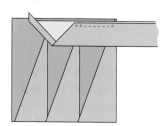

2 Starting at the centre of one of the long edges, place the doubled binding on to the right side of the quilt keeping raw edges level. Stitch the binding in place starting ¼in (6mm) in from the diagonal folded edge (see above). Reverse stitch to secure, and working ¼in (6mm) in from edge of the quilt towards first corner of quilt. Stop ¼in (6mm) in from corner and work a few reverse stitches.

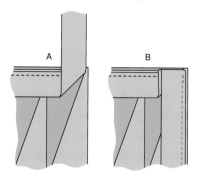

3 Fold the loose end of the binding up, making a 45-degree angle (see A). Keeping the diagonal fold in place, fold the binding back down, aligning the raw edges with the next side of the quilt. Starting at the point where the last stitch ended, stitch down the next side (see B).

4 Continue to stitch the binding in place around all the quilt edges in this way, tucking the finishing end

of the binding inside the diagonal starting section (see above).

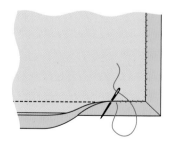

5 Turn the folded edge of the binding on to the back of the quilt. Hand stitch the folded edge in place just covering binding machine stitches, and folding a mitre at each corner.

Glossary of Terms

Appliqué The technique of stitching fabric shapes on to a background to create a design. It can be applied either by hand or machine with a decorative embroidery stitch, such as buttonhole, or satin stitch.

Backing The bottom layer of a *quilt sandwich*. It is made of fabric pieced to the size of the quilt top with the addition of about 3in (7.5cm) all around to allow for quilting take-up.

Basting or Tacking This is a means of holding two fabric layers or the layers of a *quilt sandwich* together temporarily with large hand stitches, or pins.

Batting or Wadding This is the middle layer, or *padding* in a quilt. It can be made of cotton, wool, silk or synthetic fibres.

Bias The diagonal *grain* of a fabric. This is the direction which has the most give or stretch, making it ideal for bindings, especially on curved edges.

Binding A narrow strip of fabric used to finish off the edges of quilts or projects; it can be cut on the straight *grain* of a fabric or on the *bias*.

Block A single design unit that when stitched together with other blocks create the quilt top. It is most often a square, hexagon, or rectangle, but it can be any shape. It can be pieced or plain.

Border A frame of fabric stitched to the outer edges of the quilt top. Borders can be narrow or wide, pieced or plain. As well as making the quilt larger, they unify the overall design and draw attention to the central area.

Chalk pencils Available in various colours, they are used for marking lines, or spots on fabric.

Cutting mat Designed for use with a *rotary cutter*, it is made from a special 'self-healing' material that keeps your cutting blade sharp. Cutting mats come in various sizes and are usually marked with a grid to help you line up the edges of fabric and cut out larger pieces.

Free-motion quilting Curved wavy quilting lines stitched in a random manner. Stitching diagrams are often given for you to follow as a loose guide.

Fussy cutting This is when a template is placed on a particular motif, or stripe, to obtain interesting effects. This method is not as efficient as strip cutting, but yields very interesting results.

Grain The direction in which the threads run in a woven fabric. In a vertical direction it is called the lengthwise grain, which has very little stretch. The horizontal direction, or crosswise grain is slightly stretchy, but diagonally the fabric has a lot of stretch. This grain is called the *bias*. Wherever possible the grain of a fabric should run in the same direction on a quilt *block* and *borders*.

Inset seams or setting-in A patchwork technique whereby one patch (or block) is stitched into a 'V' shape formed by the joining of two other patches (or blocks).

Patch A small shaped piece of fabric used in the making of a *patchwork* pattern.

Patchwork The technique of stitching small pieces of fabric (*patches*) together to create a larger piece of fabric, usually forming a design.

Pieced quilt A quilt composed of *patches*.

Quilting Traditionally done by hand with running stitches, but for speed modern quilts are often stitched by machine. The stitches are sewn through the top, *wadding* and *backing* to hold the three layers together. Quilting stitches are usually worked in some form of design, but they can be random.

Quilting hoop Consists of two wooden circular or oval rings with a screw adjuster on the outer ring. It stabilises the quilt layers, helping to create an even tension.

Rotary cutter A sharp circular blade attached to a handle for quick, accurate cutting. It is a device that can be used to cut up to six layers of fabric at one time. It must be used in conjunction with a 'self-healing' *cutting mat* and a thick plastic *ruler*.

Rotary ruler A thick, clear plastic ruler printed with lines that are exactly ?in (6mm) apart. Sometimes they also have diagonal lines printed on, indicating 45 and 60-degree angles. A rotary ruler is used as a guide when cutting out fabric pieces using a *rotary cutter*.

Sashing A piece or pieced sections of fabric interspaced between blocks.

Sashing Posts When blocks have sashing between them the corner squares are known as sashing posts.

Selvedges Also known as *selvages*, these are the firmly woven edges down each side of a fabric length. Selvedges should be trimmed off before cutting out your fabric, as they are more liable to shrink when the fabric is washed.

Stitch-in-the-ditch or Ditch quilting Also known as quilting-in-the-ditch. The quilting stitches are worked along the actual seam lines, to give a *pieced quilt* texture.

Template A pattern piece used as a guide for marking and cutting out fabric *patches*, or marking a *quilting*, or *appliqué* design. Usually made from plastic or strong card that can be reused many times.

Threads One hundred percent cotton or cotton-covered polyester is best for hand and machine piecing. Choose a colour that matches your fabric. When sewing different colours and patterns together, choose a medium to light neutral colour, such as grey or ecru. Specialist quilting threads are available for hand and machine quilting.

Walking foot or Quilting foot This is a sewing machine foot with dual feed control. It is very helpful when quilting, as the fabric layers are fed evenly from the top and below, reducing the risk of slippage and puckering.

Experience Ratings

★ Easy, straightforward, suitable for a beginner.

★ ★ Suitable for the average pachworker and quilter.

★ ★ ★ For the more experienced patchworker and quilter.

Printed Fabrics

When ordering printed fabrics please note the following codes which precede the fabric number and two digit colour code.

GP is the code for the Kaffe Fassett collection

CM is the code for the Carla Miller collection

LC is the code for the Lille collection

MN is the code for the Martha Negley collection

DW is the code for the David Wolverson collection

PJ is the code for the Philip Jacobs collection

The fabric collection can be viewed online at the following
www.westminsterfibers.com

Other ROWAN Titles Available

Patchwork and Quilting Book Number Four

A Colourful Journey

Kaffe Fassett's Caravan of Quilts

Kaffe Fassett's Quilt Road

Seven Easy Pieces

Rowan Living Book One

The Impatient Patchworker

The Impatient Embroiderer

All Drima and Sylko machine threads, Anchor embroidery threads, and Prym sewing aids, distributed in UK by Coats Crafts UK, P.O. Box 22, Lingfield House, Lingfield Point, McMullen Road, Darlington, Co. Durham, DL1 1YQ.
Consumer helpline: 01325 394237.
Anchor embroidery thread and Coats sewing threads, distributed in the USA by Coats & Clark,
4135 South Stream Blvd, Charlotte,
North Carolina 28217. Tel: 704 329 5016.
Fax: 704 329 5027.
Prym products distributed in the USA by Prym-Dritz Corp,
950 Brisack Road, Spartanburg, SC 29303.
Tel: +1 864 576 5050, Fax: +1 864 587 3353,
e-mail: pdmar@teleplex.net

R O W A N

Green Lane Mill, Holmfirth, West Yorkshire, England
Tel: +44 (0) 1484 681881   Fax: +44 (0) 1484 687920   Internet: www.knitrowan.com
Email: mail@knitrowan.com

Biographies

Pauline Smith

Pauline Smith has been a quilt maker since a college visit to The American Museum in Bath in 1968. With a successful business designing, making and selling patchwork through exhibition and commissions she has been involved in the development of patchwork at Rowan since 1998. Pauline designs by playing with the fabrics until she is happy with how they work together. During this process ideas for the quilt design emerge.

As the Rowan patchwork co-ordinator, she works closely with Kaffe Fassett and everyone involved in producing the 'Patchwork and Quilting' series.

Ruth Eglington

Ruth's first job was in banking, and her ability with numbers, computers and organisation was born there. After getting married, she took up dressmaking for her little girls and it was during a shopping trip for fabric that she met her great friend Maggie Wise. Maggie was the catalyst that launched Ruth into the quilting world. After a while Ruth discovered the 'mathematics' of quilt making is her real flair and embarked on a new career in technical editing and illustrating combining her ability with computers, with her love of all things fabric. She first worked with a British quilting magazine, then for the last 5 years with Rowan.

Liza Prior Lucy

Liza Prior Lucy first began making quilts in 1990. She was so enthralled by the craftspeople she met and by the generously stocked quilt fabric shops in the States that quiltmaking soon became a passion. Liza originally trained as a knitwear designer and produced features for needlework magazines. She also owned and operated her own needlepoint shop in Washington, D.C. Liza met Kaffe when she was working as a sales representative for Rowan Yarns in the New York City area - Kaffe had come to America to promote his books and was working as Rowan's leading designer. They worked closely together in the States and the UK to write and produce the quilts for the books Glorious Patchwork and Passionate Patchwork.

Roberta Horton

Roberta Horton of Berkeley, California has been a quiltmaker for over 30 years. She has taught and lectured worldwide. Her study and love of quilts has pushed her into developing many workshops and to the authoring of six books. Roberta was the recipient of the 2000 Silver Star Award presented by the International Quilt Assosiation. This was in recognition of her lifetime body of work and the long-term effect it has had on quilting.

Brandon Mably

A regular contributor to the Rowan Patchwork books Brandon Mably has built a reputation as a quilt designer of simple, elegant quilts in restful colours. Brandon trained at The Kaffe Fassett Studio. He designs for the Rowan and Vogue Knitting magazine knitwear collections, and is the author of 'Brilliant Knits'.

Mary Mashuta

California quiltmaker Mary Mashuta has been making quilts and wearables for over thirty years. She is a professionally trained teacher who has been teaching internationally since 1985. Her classes always stress easily understood colour and design. She knows that no quilter can own too much fabric, and she enjoys discovering new blocks to showcase personal collections.

Mary has authored five books and numerous magazine articles. To find out more about Mary read 'Fabric & Colour Too Much Is Not Enough' on page 46.

Distributors and Stockists

Overseas Distributors of Rowan Fabrics

AUSTRALIA
XLN Fabrics
2/21 Binney Road,
Kings Park
New South Wales 2148
Tel: 61 2 96213066

CANADA
Westminster Fibers Inc
4 Townsend West
Suite 8,
Nashua
New Hampshire 03063
Tel: 1 603 886 5041
Fax: 1 603 886 1056
E-mail: rowan@westminsterfibers.com

BELGIUM
Rhinetex
Geurdeland 7
6673 DR Andelst
Tel: 31 488 480030
Fax: 31 488 480422
E-mail: info@rhinetex.com

DENMARK
Coats Danmark A/S
Marienlundsalle 4
7430 Ikast
Danmark
Tel: +45 9660 3400
Fax: +45 9660 3408
Email: coats@coats.dk

FINLAND
Coats Opti Oy
Ketjutie 3
04220 Kerava
Tel: 358 9 274 871
Fax: 358 9 2748 7330
E-mail: coatsoptisales@coats.com

FRANCE
Rhinetex
Geurdeland 7
6673 DR Andelst
Tel: 31 488 480030
Fax: 31 488 480422
E-mail: info@rhinetex.com

GERMANY
Rhinetex
Geurdeland 7
6673 DR Andelst
Tel: 31 488 480030
Fax: 31 488 480422
E-mail: info@rhinetex.com

HOLLAND
Rhinetex
Geurdeland 7
6673 DR Andelst
Tel: 31 488 480030
Fax: 31 488 480422
E-mail: info@rhinetex.com

ICELAND
Storkurinn
Laugavegi 59
101 Reykjavik
Tel: 354 551 8258
Fax: 354 562 8252
E-mail: malin@mmedia.is

ITALY
D.L SRL
Via Piave 24 - 26
20016 PERO
MILANO
Tel: 39 02 339 10 180
Fax: 39 02 339 14661

JAPAN
Yokota & Co Ltd
5-14 2 Chome Minamikyuhoojimachi
Chuo-Ku
OSAKA
Tel: 81 6 6251 7179

NEW ZEALAND
Fabco Limited
PO Box 84-002
Westgate
AUCKLAND 1250
Tel: 64 9 411 9996
Fax: 64 9 411 9506
E mail: info@fabco.co.nz

NORWAY
Coats Knappehuset AS
Boks 100 Ulset
5873 Bergen
Norway
Tel: (47) 555 39 300
Fax: (47) 555 39 393
Email: post@knappehuset.no

SOUTH KOREA
Coats Korea Co Ltd,
5F Kuckdong B/D, 935-40
Bangbae- Dong,
Seocho-Gu, Seoul.
Tel: (82) 2 521 6262
Fax: (82) 2 521 5181

SOUTH AFRICA
Arthur Bales PTY Ltd
PO Box 44644
Linden 2104
Tel: 27 11 888 2401
Fax: 27 11 782 6137
E-mail: arthurb@new.co.za

SPAIN
Lucretia Beleta Patchwork
Dr Rizal 12
08006 Barcelona
Tel: 34 93 41 59555
Fax: 34 9341 55241
E-mail: lucrecia@lbpatchwork.com

SWITZERLAND
Rhinetex
Geurdeland 7
6673 DR Andelst
Tel: 31 488 480030
Fax: 31 488 480422
E-mail: info@rhinetex.com

SWEDEN
Coats Expotex AB
Division Craft
J.A. Wettergrens Gata 7
42130 Vastra Froulunda
Sweden
Tel: 46 33 720 79 10
Fax: 46 33 720 79 40
E-mail: info.kundtjänst@coatscraft.se

TAIWAN
Long Teh Trading Co
6F #156, Shifu Road
Taichung City
Tel: 886 4 2225 6698
Fax: 886 4 2225 6697

UK
Rowan
Green Lane Mill
Holmfirth
West Yorkshire
England, HD9 2DX
Tel: +44(0) 1484 681881
Internet: www.knitrowan.com
Email: mail@knitrowan.com

U.S.A
Westminster Fibers Inc
4 Townsend West
Suite 8,
Nashua
New Hampshire 03063
Tel: 1 603 886 5041
Fax: 1 603 886 1056
E-mail: rowan@westminsterfibers.com